VOICES OF OUR REPUBLIC

VOICES OF OUR REPUBLIC

EXPLORING THE CONSTITUTION

WITH

Ruth Bader Ginsburg,
Alan Dershowitz,
Sandra Day O'Connor,
Ron Chernow,
and Many More

EDITED BY DOUGLAS H. GINSBURG
JUDGE, US COURT OF APPEALS, DC CIRCUIT

FOREWORD BY ROB CHATFIELD
PRODUCTION PHOTOS BY BARBARA POTTER

Skyhorse Publishing

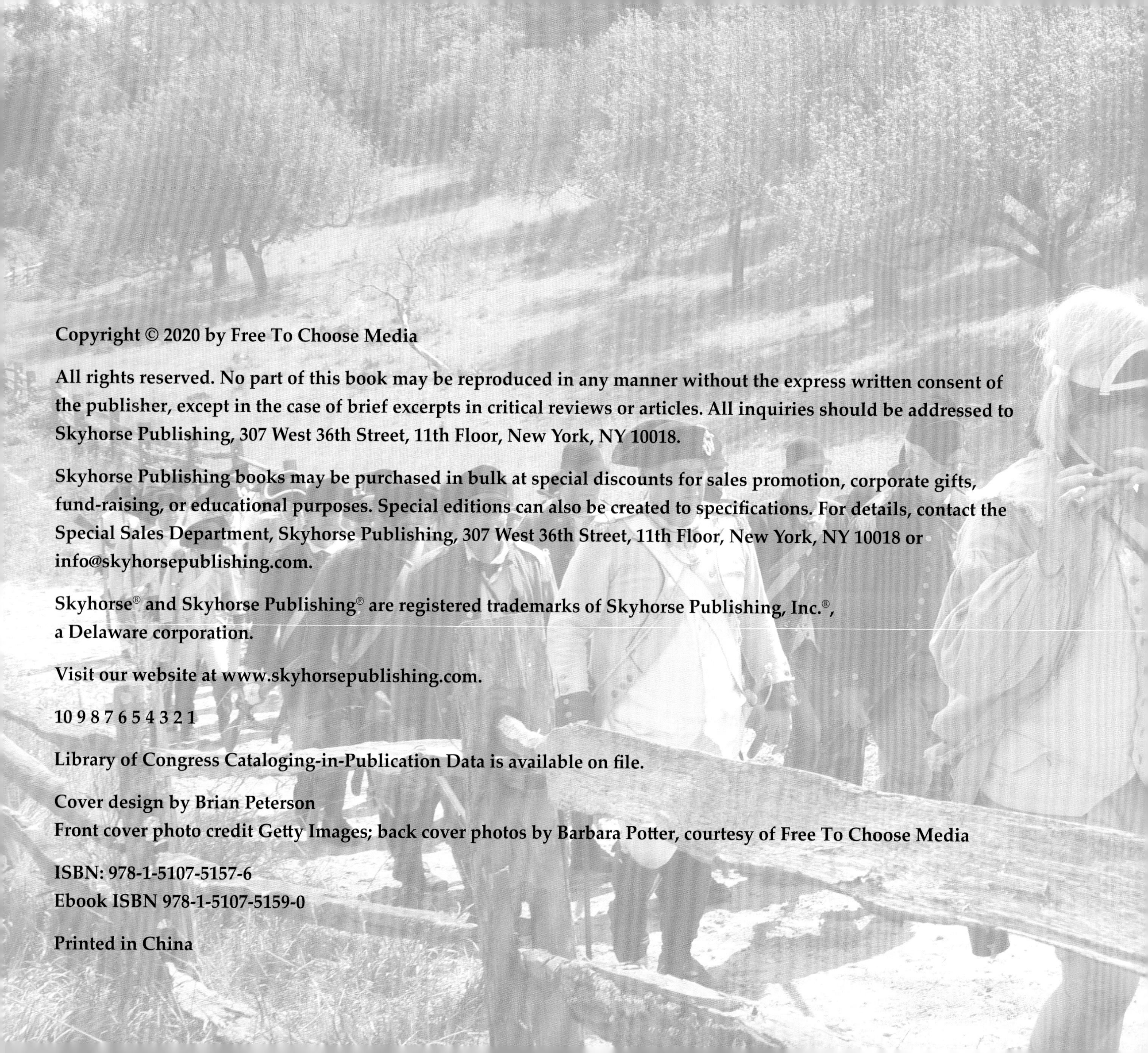

Skyhorse Publishing books may be purchased in bulk at special discounts for sales promotion, corporate gifts, fund-raising, or educational purposes. Special editions can also be created to specifications. For details, contact the Special Sales Department, Skyhorse Publishing, 307 West 36th Street, 11th Floor, New York, NY 10018 or info@skyhorsepublishing.com.

Visit our website at www.skyhorsepublishing.com.

10 9 8 7 6 5 4 3 2 1

Library of Congress Cataloging-in-Publication Data is available on file.

Cover design by Brian Peterson
Front cover photo credit Getty Images; back cover photos by Barbara Potter, courtesy of Free To Choose Media

ISBN: 978-1-5107-5157-6
Ebook ISBN 978-1-5107-5159-0

Printed in China

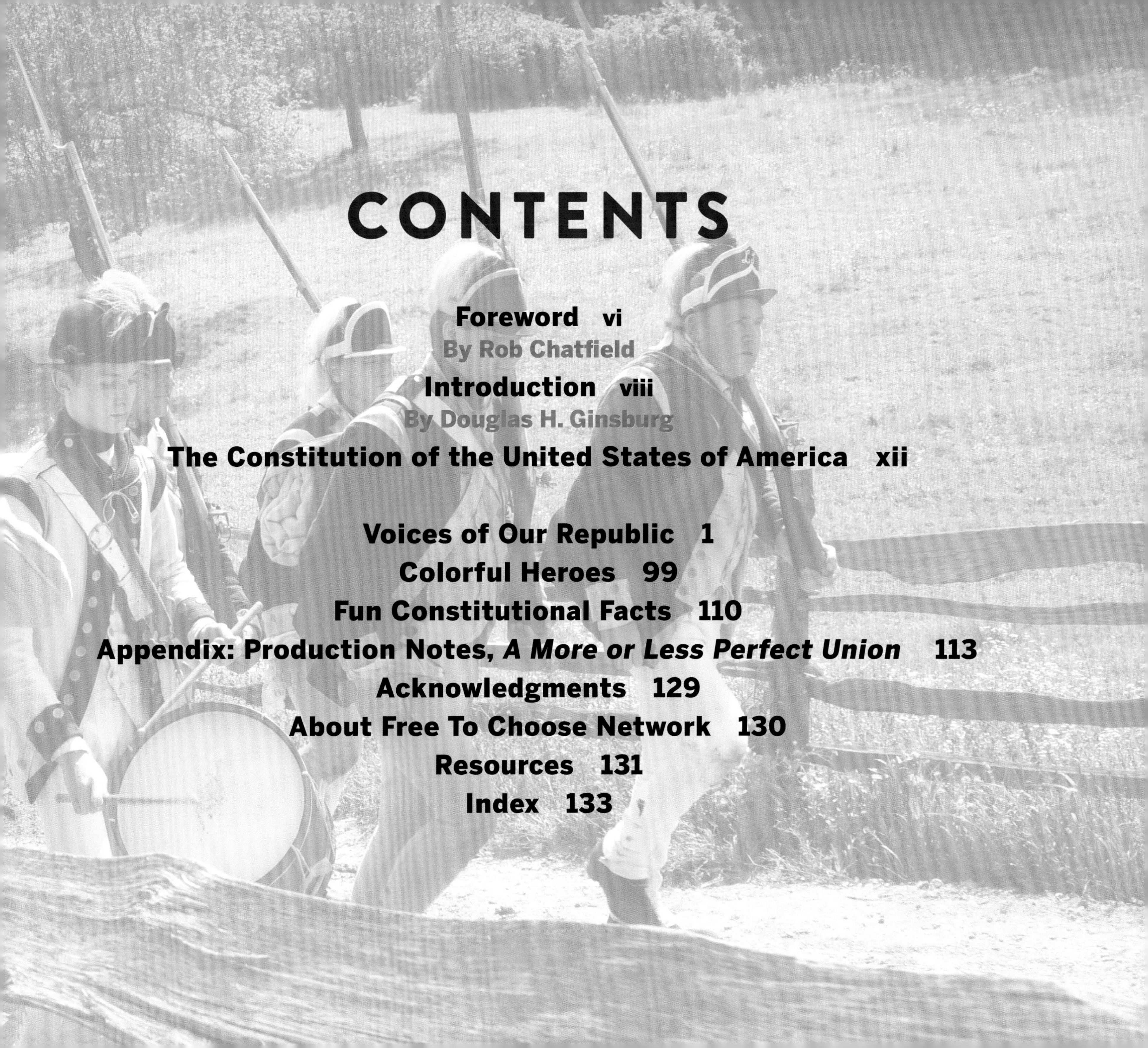

CONTENTS

FOREWORD
ROB CHATFIELD

Our system of government is not working! Or that's what I imagine the Founders were thinking while watching their country stagnate under the Articles of Confederation. That document was intended as a wartime resolution to provide some framework for a united defense. After the Revolutionary War, the system was wholly inadequate. The agreement required unanimous consent for any amendment or structural change to national government. Of the thirteen states, nine of them had to vote affirmatively to pass a law. Government relied on voluntary contributions to pay off debts incurred during the fight for independence. The system of government simply did not work.

Today, there are many who think our current system of government is not working. A partisan divide is caused by those who wish to use government to conform others to their viewpoint, but the United States was never intended as a procrustean system; the right of individuals to BE individuals has always been the defining feature of our system of government. Unanimity was never the intention and safeguards were carefully put in place to defend the right of the individual against a majority of voters.

The Constitution was never perfect. The agreement provided a framework to move forward. It took nearly eighty years to amend the Constitution to abolish slavery throughout the nation. It took another fifty-five years to grant women the right to vote. But the framework allowed for change, and nearly all changes have erred on the side of providing individuals with more—not less—freedom.

Our three-part series, *A More or Less Perfect Union*, and this companion book started as a side note to a biographical film on economics professor Walter Williams. In that film, Professor Williams laments, "Americans have lost their love for the United States Constitution" and enters into a discussion with Judge Douglas Ginsburg about where this relationship may have gone awry.

The conversation between Professor Williams and Judge Ginsburg planted the seed for a project that might serve to nourish the next generation with an important truth—that freedom is not gained or retained easily.

Enter Bob Chitester, the master video storyteller who originally brought the world Milton Friedman's ten-part television series, *Free to Choose*, in 1980. Chitester was a sprightly seventy-five-year-old filmmaker who noticed that an entire generation of Americans had not grown up in the face of the Cold War. That experience provided a unifying condition in the United States and also provided a clear understanding of what is often referred to as American exceptionalism: the notion that our nation has an imperative to defend the principles of personal, economic, and political freedom.

Chitester noticed "Us vs. Them" was being replaced by "Us vs. Us" and set about raising interest in a project that would bring these issues to the forefront of the American public. From the start, this project was intended to spark understanding, not just debate. Chitester understood the power of bringing people together to distinguish between a republic and a democracy, the rationale for the process of amending the Constitution, highlighting those things that make our system of government not only unique, but exceptional.

Judge Douglas Ginsburg was the natural choice to host the project. From the beginning, Judge Ginsburg wanted to look at the Constitution from a fresh perspective to see why people may have fallen out of love with this document. At every turn, Judge Ginsburg's soft-spoken, poignant, and insightful approach provided a lens for all Americans to see the Constitution through the eyes of the many individuals he encountered. He wanted to tackle difficult issues related to slavery and civil rights. Most important, he wanted to address the areas where our nation is at risk without a clear understanding of the Constitution.

Producer Barbara Potter and director Jim Taylor gathered legal scholars, unsung heroes, and people on the street to present a wide-ranging view of the Constitution. As they neared completion of editing some 135 hours of footage into a three-hour television series, we started hearing from some well-known people that they might like to participate in the project. People like Gregory Fenves, president of the University of Texas at Austin, a descendant of a Nazi concentration camp survivor. People like General Ann Dunwoody and Olympian Jackie Joyner-Kersee, who reflect on patriotism from a sense of unity.

Voices of Our Republic provides an opportunity for We the People to hear from some of these familiar faces, some people featured in the documentary film, and hopefully a few faces that will make you ask, "Who is . . .?" After all, this melting pot of individuals is what makes America exceptional.

Rob Chatfield is President / CEO of Free To Choose Network

"The conversation between Professor Williams and Judge Ginsburg planted the seed for a project that might serve to nourish the next generation with an important truth—that freedom is not gained or retained easily."

INTRODUCTION

DOUGLAS H. GINSBURG

JUDGE, US COURT OF APPEALS, DC CIRCUIT

The Constitution of the United States means many different things to many different people. For those of us born here, the Constitution may be a source of comfort, knowing we are protected from arbitrary government. To newly naturalized citizens, it embodies an ideal of freedom for which they have made great sacrifices, leaving their homes and friends behind. And we all can be proud that many other countries have taken our Constitution as a model for their own.

We asked a number of people prominent in American life what the Constitution means to them. They come from many different backgrounds and have had a wide array of careers and life experiences. Unsurprisingly, they gave us a great variety of well-considered thoughts and insights. Running through that variety, however, is a consistent sense of the centrality of the Constitution in American life. In a big and diverse country, which the United States has been from the moment of its founding, the Constitution is what unites us. As Alan Kors has said, unlike other countries, "We don't have an ethnicity, we don't have a religion, we have a constitution." And as Jonathan Rauch has pointed out, "What we do when we become Americans is not swear an oath of allegiance to the United States of America, or to the existing government of America; we swear an oath to the Constitution. It unites us and makes us a country."

It has rightly been said that this country is unique in the world because it was founded on an idea, the idea that a people could govern themselves. The people would be the masters and the government would be the servant, not the other way around. And so the Constitution provided.

Unfortunately, not every American gives much thought to the Constitution. Too many of us take our liberties for granted. In a 2017 survey, 37 percent could not identify a single First Amendment right. Fewer than half named freedom of speech, and fewer still identified freedom of religion (15%), the press (14%), assembly (10%), or petition (3%). Civics is no longer widely enough taught in our primary and secondary schools.[1] But it is never too late for a citizen to study the Constitution. My own love affair with the Constitution did not begin until college and did not mature into a lifelong relationship until I was in law school.

A great deal has changed—in the country and in the Constitution itself—since the Constitution was drafted in 1787 and ratified by the states in 1789. The country has grown from a largely agrarian society in the confines of the eastern seaboard

1 Annenberg Public Policy Center, University of Pennsylvania, https://www.annenbergpublicpolicycenter.org/americans-are-poorly-informed-about-basic-constitutional-provisions/

Best Wishes

> "This country is unique in the world because it was founded on an idea, the idea that a people could govern themselves."

to a great, urbanized power spanning the continent. And the Constitution has been amended twenty-seven times, first in 1791 by the ten amendments known as the Bill of Rights, and most recently by the Twenty-seventh Amendment, which had been proposed as part of the Bill of Rights, but was not ratified by the states until 201 years later, in 1992. In between came the Civil War Amendments to secure the rights of the newly freed slaves; amendments extending the right to vote to women and then to eighteen-year-olds; an amendment allowing a federal income tax; and amendments bringing in and, a mere fourteen years later, ushering out Prohibition.

The Constitution has also been "interpreted" by the Supreme Court to make certain clauses meaningless and to give other clauses new meaning. That evolution at the hands of the Court has been celebrated by many as a testament to the needed flexibility of the Constitution to respond to new circumstances, and lamented by others, myself included, as a betrayal of the ideals and principles that animated the Constitution in the first place.

It also gave rise to the debate initiated in 1985 by Attorney General Edwin Meese III and Justice William J. Brennan: Original Meaning vs. A Living Constitution. Should a court read the words of the Constitution as those who wrote and ratified them understood them? Or is a court authorized to give those words a new and different meaning in response to new and different circumstances? For example, does "due process" refer, as it did at the Founding, to the procedures to which one is entitled by law and custom before the government can take your life, liberty, or property? Or does it have a "substantive component," as the Supreme Court has said, that imports into the Constitution rights unrelated to procedure but deemed important by the Court? Or consider the Fifth Amendment, one part of which provides that, so long as the owner is justly compensated, private property may be taken "for public use," typical examples being to build a road or a post office. Not long ago, however, the Supreme Court read that provision to require only a "public purpose," so property could be taken from one person and given to another to build an office building as part of an urban renewal plan. But a purpose is not a use. The Rule of Law demands greater fidelity to the words so carefully chosen by the Framers of the Constitution. As Margaret Thatcher said to me (and no doubt others), "The rule of law was Britain's great gift to the world." To squander so precious an inheritance would be more than tragic; it would be disastrous for liberty.

Lewis Carroll grasped the issue in his sequel to *Alice in Wonderland*: "When I use a word," Humpty Dumpty said, in rather a scornful tone, "it means just what I choose it to mean—neither more nor less." "The question is," said Alice, "whether you can make words mean so many different things." "The question is," said Humpty Dumpty, "which is to be master—that's all." So, which is to be *our* master—the Constitution or the Court?

In this volume, more than seventy-five thoughtful and influential people share their views on this and other vital questions surrounding our Constitution.

Read on, see what they have to say, and decide for yourself what the Constitution means to you.

THE CONSTITUTION OF THE UNITED STATES OF AMERICA

We the People of the United States, in Order to form a more perfect Union, establish Justice, insure domestic Tranquility, provide for the common defence, promote the general Welfare, and secure the Blessings of Liberty to ourselves and our Posterity, do ordain and establish this Constitution for the United States of America.

Article. I.

Section. 1.

All legislative Powers herein granted shall be vested in a Congress of the United States, which shall consist of a Senate and House of Representatives.

Section. 2.

The House of Representatives shall be composed of Members chosen every second Year by the People of the several States, and the Electors in each State shall have the Qualifications requisite for Electors of the most numerous Branch of the State Legislature.

No Person shall be a Representative who shall not have attained to the Age of twenty five Years, and been seven Years a Citizen of the United States, and who shall not, when elected, be an Inhabitant of that State in which he shall be chosen.

Representatives and direct Taxes shall be apportioned among the several States which may be included within this Union, according to their respective Numbers, which shall be determined by adding to the whole Number of free Persons, including those bound to Service for a Term of Years, and excluding Indians not taxed, three fifths of all other Persons. The actual Enumeration shall be made within three Years after the first Meeting of the Congress of the United States, and within every subsequent Term of ten Years, in such Manner as they shall by Law direct. The Number of Representatives shall not exceed one for every thirty Thousand, but each State shall have at Least one Representative; and until such enumeration shall be made, the State of New Hampshire shall be entitled to chuse three, Massachusetts eight, Rhode-Island and Providence Plantations one, Connecticut five, New-York six, New Jersey four, Pennsylvania eight, Delaware one, Maryland six, Virginia ten, North Carolina five, South Carolina five, and Georgia three.

When vacancies happen in the Representation from any State, the Executive Authority thereof shall issue Writs of Election to fill such Vacancies.

The House of Representatives shall chuse their Speaker and other Officers; and shall have the sole Power of Impeachment.

Section. 3.

The Senate of the United States shall be composed of two Senators from each State, chosen by the Legislature thereof, for six Years; and each Senator shall have one Vote.

Immediately after they shall be assembled in Consequence of the first Election, they shall be divided as equally as may be into three Classes. The Seats of the Senators of the first Class shall be vacated at the Expiration of the second Year, of the second Class at the Expiration of the fourth Year, and of the third Class at the Expiration of the sixth Year, so that one third may be chosen every second Year; and if Vacancies happen by Resignation, or otherwise, during the Recess of the Legislature of any State, the Executive thereof may make temporary Appointments until the next Meeting of the Legislature, which shall then fill such Vacancies.

No Person shall be a Senator who shall not have attained to the Age of thirty Years, and been nine Years a Citizen of the United States, and who shall not, when elected, be an Inhabitant of that State for which he shall be chosen.

The Vice President of the United States shall be President of the Senate, but shall have no Vote, unless they be equally divided.

The Senate shall chuse their other Officers, and also a President pro tempore, in the Absence of the Vice President, or when he shall exercise the Office of President of the United States.

The Senate shall have the sole Power to try all Impeachments. When sitting for that Purpose, they shall be on Oath or Affirmation. When the President of the United States is tried, the Chief Justice shall preside: And no Person shall be convicted without the Concurrence of two thirds of the Members present.

Judgment in Cases of Impeachment shall not extend further than to removal from Office, and disqualification to hold and enjoy any Office of honor, Trust or Profit under the United States: but the Party convicted shall nevertheless be liable and subject to Indictment, Trial, Judgment and Punishment, according to Law.

Section. 4.

The Times, Places and Manner of holding Elections for Senators and Representatives, shall be prescribed in each State by the Legislature thereof; but the Congress may at any time by Law make or alter such Regulations, except as to the Places of chusing Senators.

The Congress shall assemble at least once in every Year, and such Meeting shall be on the first Monday in December, unless they shall by Law appoint a different Day.

Section. 5.

Each House shall be the Judge of the Elections, Returns and Qualifications of its own Members, and a Majority of each shall constitute a Quorum to do Business; but a smaller Number may adjourn from day to day, and may be authorized to compel the Attendance of absent Members, in such Manner, and under such Penalties as each House may provide.

Each House may determine the Rules of its Proceedings, punish its Members for disorderly Behaviour, and, with the Concurrence of two thirds, expel a Member.

Each House shall keep a Journal of its Proceedings, and from time to time publish the same, excepting such Parts as may in their Judgment require Secrecy; and the Yeas and Nays of the Members of either House on any question shall, at the Desire of one fifth of those Present, be entered on the Journal.

Neither House, during the Session of Congress, shall, without the Consent of the other, adjourn for more than three days, nor to any other Place than that in which the two Houses shall be sitting.

Section. 6.

The Senators and Representatives shall receive a Compensation for their Services, to be ascertained by Law, and paid out of the Treasury of the United States. They shall in all Cases, except Treason, Felony and Breach of the Peace, be privileged from Arrest during their Attendance at the Session of their respective Houses, and in going to and returning from the same; and for any

Speech or Debate in either House, they shall not be questioned in any other Place.

No Senator or Representative shall, during the Time for which he was elected, be appointed to any civil Office under the Authority of the United States, which shall have been created, or the Emoluments whereof shall have been encreased during such time; and no Person holding any Office under the United States, shall be a Member of either House during his Continuance in Office.

Section. 7.

All Bills for raising Revenue shall originate in the House of Representatives; but the Senate may propose or concur with Amendments as on other Bills.

Every Bill which shall have passed the House of Representatives and the Senate, shall, before it become a Law, be presented to the President of the United States; If he approve he shall sign it, but if not he shall return it, with his Objections to that House in which it shall have originated, who shall enter the Objections at large on their Journal, and proceed to reconsider it. If after such Reconsideration two thirds of that House shall agree to pass the Bill, it shall be sent, together with the Objections, to the other House, by which it shall likewise be reconsidered, and if approved by two thirds of that House, it shall become a Law. But in all such Cases the Votes of both Houses shall be determined by yeas and Nays, and the Names of the Persons voting for and against the Bill shall be entered on the Journal of each House respectively. If any Bill shall not be returned by the President within ten Days (Sundays excepted) after it shall have been presented to him, the Same shall be a Law, in like Manner as if he had signed it, unless the Congress by their Adjournment prevent its Return, in which Case it shall not be a Law.

Every Order, Resolution, or Vote to which the Concurrence of the Senate and House of Representatives may be necessary (except on a question of Adjournment) shall be presented to the President of the United States; and before the Same shall take Effect, shall be approved by him, or being disapproved by him, shall be repassed by two thirds of the Senate and House of Representatives, according to the Rules and Limitations prescribed in the Case of a Bill.

Section. 8.

The Congress shall have Power To lay and collect Taxes, Duties, Imposts and Excises, to pay the Debts and provide for the common Defence and general Welfare of the United States; but all Duties, Imposts and Excises shall be uniform throughout the United States;

To borrow Money on the credit of the United States;

To regulate Commerce with foreign Nations, and among the several States, and with the Indian Tribes;

To establish an uniform Rule of Naturalization, and uniform Laws on the subject of Bankruptcies throughout the United States;

To coin Money, regulate the Value thereof, and of foreign Coin, and fix the Standard of Weights and Measures;

To provide for the Punishment of counterfeiting the Securities and current Coin of the United States;

To establish Post Offices and post Roads;

To promote the Progress of Science and useful Arts, by securing for limited Times to Authors and Inventors the exclusive Right to their respective Writings and Discoveries;

To constitute Tribunals inferior to the supreme Court;

To define and punish Piracies and Felonies committed on the high Seas, and Offences against the Law of Nations;

To declare War, grant Letters of Marque and Reprisal, and make Rules concerning Captures on Land and Water;

To raise and support Armies, but no Appropriation of Money to that Use shall be for a longer Term than two Years;

To provide and maintain a Navy;

To make Rules for the Government and Regulation of the land and naval Forces;

To provide for calling forth the Militia to execute the Laws of the Union, suppress Insurrections and repel Invasions;

To provide for organizing, arming, and disciplining, the

Militia, and for governing such Part of them as may be employed in the Service of the United States, reserving to the States respectively, the Appointment of the Officers, and the Authority of training the Militia according to the discipline prescribed by Congress;

To exercise exclusive Legislation in all Cases whatsoever, over such District (not exceeding ten Miles square) as may, by Cession of particular States, and the Acceptance of Congress, become the Seat of the Government of the United States, and to exercise like Authority over all Places purchased by the Consent of the Legislature of the State in which the Same shall be, for the Erection of Forts, Magazines, Arsenals, dock-Yards, and other needful Buildings;—And

To make all Laws which shall be necessary and proper for carrying into Execution the foregoing Powers, and all other Powers vested by this Constitution in the Government of the United States, or in any Department or Officer thereof.

Section. 9.

The Migration or Importation of such Persons as any of the States now existing shall think proper to admit, shall not be prohibited by the Congress prior to the Year one thousand eight hundred and eight, but a Tax or duty may be imposed on such Importation, not exceeding ten dollars for each Person.

The Privilege of the Writ of Habeas Corpus shall not be suspended, unless when in Cases of Rebellion or Invasion the public Safety may require it.

No Bill of Attainder or ex post facto Law shall be passed.

No Capitation, or other direct, Tax shall be laid, unless in Proportion to the Census or enumeration herein before directed to be taken.

No Tax or Duty shall be laid on Articles exported from any State.

No Preference shall be given by any Regulation of Commerce or Revenue to the Ports of one State over those of another: nor shall Vessels bound to, or from, one State, be obliged to enter, clear, or pay Duties in another.

No Money shall be drawn from the Treasury, but in Consequence of Appropriations made by Law; and a regular Statement and Account of the Receipts and Expenditures of all public Money shall be published from time to time.

No Title of Nobility shall be granted by the United States: And no Person holding any Office of Profit or Trust under them, shall, without the Consent of the Congress, accept of any present, Emolument, Office, or Title, of any kind whatever, from any King, Prince, or foreign State.

Section. 10.

No State shall enter into any Treaty, Alliance, or Confederation; grant Letters of Marque and Reprisal; coin Money; emit Bills of Credit; make any Thing but gold and silver Coin a Tender in Payment of Debts; pass any Bill of Attainder, ex post facto Law, or Law impairing the Obligation of Contracts, or grant any Title of Nobility.

No State shall, without the Consent of the Congress, lay any Imposts or Duties on Imports or Exports, except what may be absolutely necessary for executing it's inspection Laws: and the net Produce of all Duties and Imposts, laid by any State on Imports or Exports, shall be for the Use of the Treasury of the United States; and all such Laws shall be subject to the Revision and Controul of the Congress.

No State shall, without the Consent of Congress, lay any Duty of Tonnage, keep Troops, or Ships of War in time of Peace, enter into any Agreement or Compact with another State, or with a foreign Power, or engage in War, unless actually invaded, or in such imminent Danger as will not admit of delay.

Article. II.

Section. 1.

The executive Power shall be vested in a President of the United States of America. He shall hold his Office during the Term of four Years, and, together with the Vice President, chosen for the same Term, be elected, as follows

Each State shall appoint, in such Manner as the Legislature

thereof may direct, a Number of Electors, equal to the whole Number of Senators and Representatives to which the State may be entitled in the Congress: but no Senator or Representative, or Person holding an Office of Trust or Profit under the United States, shall be appointed an Elector.

The Electors shall meet in their respective States, and vote by Ballot for two Persons, of whom one at least shall not be an Inhabitant of the same State with themselves. And they shall make a List of all the Persons voted for, and of the Number of Votes for each; which List they shall sign and certify, and transmit sealed to the Seat of the Government of the United States, directed to the President of the Senate. The President of the Senate shall, in the Presence of the Senate and House of Representatives, open all the Certificates, and the Votes shall then be counted. The Person having the greatest Number of Votes shall be the President, if such Number be a Majority of the whole Number of Electors appointed; and if there be more than one who have such Majority, and have an equal Number of Votes, then the House of Representatives shall immediately chuse by Ballot one of them for President; and if no Person have a Majority, then from the five highest on the List the said House shall in like Manner chuse the President. But in chusing the President, the Votes shall be taken by States, the Representation from each State having one Vote; A quorum for this Purpose shall consist of a Member or Members from two thirds of the States, and a Majority of all the States shall be necessary to a Choice. In every Case, after the Choice of the President, the Person having the greatest Number of Votes of the Electors shall be the Vice President. But if there should remain two or more who have equal Votes, the Senate shall chuse from them by Ballot the Vice President.

The Congress may determine the Time of chusing the Electors, and the Day on which they shall give their Votes; which Day shall be the same throughout the United States.

No Person except a natural born Citizen, or a Citizen of the United States, at the time of the Adoption of this Constitution, shall be eligible to the Office of President; neither shall any Person be eligible to that Office who shall not have attained to the Age of thirty five Years, and been fourteen Years a Resident within the United States.

In Case of the Removal of the President from Office, or of his Death, Resignation, or Inability to discharge the Powers and Duties of the said Office, the Same shall devolve on the Vice President, and the Congress may by Law provide for the Case of Removal, Death, Resignation or Inability, both of the President and Vice President, declaring what Officer shall then act as President, and such Officer shall act accordingly, until the Disability be removed, or a President shall be elected.

The President shall, at stated Times, receive for his Services, a Compensation, which shall neither be encreased nor diminished during the Period for which he shall have been elected, and he shall not receive within that Period any other Emolument from the United States, or any of them.

Before he enter on the Execution of his Office, he shall take the following Oath or Affirmation:—"I do solemnly swear (or affirm) that I will faithfully execute the Office of President of the United States, and will to the best of my Ability, preserve, protect and defend the Constitution of the United States."

Section. 2.

The President shall be Commander in Chief of the Army and Navy of the United States, and of the Militia of the several States, when called into the actual Service of the United States; he may require the Opinion, in writing, of the principal Officer in each of the executive Departments, upon any Subject relating to the Duties of their respective Offices, and he shall have Power to grant Reprieves and Pardons for Offences against the United States, except in Cases of Impeachment.

He shall have Power, by and with the Advice and Consent of the Senate, to make Treaties, provided two thirds of the Senators present concur; and he shall nominate, and by and with the Advice and Consent of the Senate, shall appoint Ambassadors, other public Ministers and Consuls, Judges of the supreme Court, and all other Officers of the United States, whose Appointments are not herein otherwise provided for, and which shall be established by Law: but the Congress may by Law vest the Appointment of such inferior Officers, as they think proper, in the President alone, in the Courts of Law, or in the Heads of Departments.

The President shall have Power to fill up all Vacancies that may happen during the Recess of the Senate, by granting Commissions which shall expire at the End of their next Session.

Section. 3.

He shall from time to time give to the Congress Information of the State of the Union, and recommend to their Consideration such Measures as he shall judge necessary and expedient; he may, on extraordinary Occasions, convene both Houses, or either of them, and in Case of Disagreement between them, with Respect to the Time of Adjournment, he may adjourn them to such Time as he shall think proper; he shall receive Ambassadors and other public Ministers; he shall take Care that the Laws be faithfully executed, and shall Commission all the Officers of the United States.

Section. 4.

The President, Vice President and all civil Officers of the United States, shall be removed from Office on Impeachment for, and Conviction of, Treason, Bribery, or other high Crimes and Misdemeanors.

Article III.

Section. 1.

The judicial Power of the United States, shall be vested in one supreme Court, and in such inferior Courts as the Congress may from time to time ordain and establish. The Judges, both of the supreme and inferior Courts, shall hold their Offices during good Behaviour, and shall, at stated Times, receive for their Services, a Compensation, which shall not be diminished during their Continuance in Office.

Section. 2.

The judicial Power shall extend to all Cases, in Law and Equity, arising under this Constitution, the Laws of the United States, and Treaties made, or which shall be made, under their Authority;—to all Cases affecting Ambassadors, other public Ministers and Consuls;—to all Cases of admiralty and maritime Jurisdiction;—to Controversies to which the United States shall be a Party;—to Controversies between two or more States;—between a State and Citizens of another State,—between Citizens of different States,—between Citizens of the same State claiming Lands under Grants of different States, and between a State, or the Citizens thereof, and foreign States, Citizens or Subjects.

In all Cases affecting Ambassadors, other public Ministers and Consuls, and those in which a State shall be Party, the supreme Court shall have original Jurisdiction. In all the other Cases before mentioned, the supreme Court shall have appellate Jurisdiction, both as to Law and Fact, with such Exceptions, and under such Regulations as the Congress shall make.

The Trial of all Crimes, except in Cases of Impeachment, shall be by Jury; and such Trial shall be held in the State where the said Crimes shall have been committed; but when not committed within any State, the Trial shall be at such Place or Places as the Congress may by Law have directed.

Section. 3.

Treason against the United States, shall consist only in levying War against them, or in adhering to their Enemies, giving them Aid and Comfort. No Person shall be convicted of Treason unless on the Testimony of two Witnesses to the same overt Act, or on Confession in open Court.

The Congress shall have Power to declare the Punishment of Treason, but no Attainder of Treason shall work Corruption of Blood, or Forfeiture except during the Life of the Person attainted.

Article. IV.

Section. 1.

Full Faith and Credit shall be given in each State to the public Acts, Records, and judicial Proceedings of every other State. And the Congress may by general Laws prescribe the Manner in which such Acts, Records and Proceedings shall be proved, and the Effect thereof.

Section. 2.

The Citizens of each State shall be entitled to all Privileges and Immunities of Citizens in the several States.

A Person charged in any State with Treason, Felony, or other Crime, who shall flee from Justice, and be found in another State, shall on Demand of the executive Authority of the State from which he fled, be delivered up, to be removed to the State having Jurisdiction of the Crime.

No Person held to Service or Labour in one State, under the Laws thereof, escaping into another, shall, in Consequence of any Law or Regulation therein, be discharged from such Service or Labour, but shall be delivered up on Claim of the Party to whom such Service or Labour may be due.

Section. 3.

New States may be admitted by the Congress into this Union; but no new State shall be formed or erected within the Jurisdiction of any other State; nor any State be formed by the Junction of two or more States, or Parts of States, without the Consent of the Legislatures of the States concerned as well as of the Congress.

The Congress shall have Power to dispose of and make all needful Rules and Regulations respecting the Territory or other Property belonging to the United States; and nothing in this Constitution shall be so construed as to Prejudice any Claims of the United States, or of any particular State.

Section. 4.

The United States shall guarantee to every State in this Union a Republican Form of Government, and shall protect each of them against Invasion; and on Application of the Legislature, or of the Executive (when the Legislature cannot be convened), against domestic Violence.

Article. V.

The Congress, whenever two thirds of both Houses shall deem it necessary, shall propose Amendments to this Constitution, or, on the Application of the Legislatures of two thirds of the several States, shall call a Convention for proposing Amendments, which, in either Case, shall be valid to all Intents and Purposes, as Part of this Constitution, when ratified by the Legislatures of three fourths of the several States, or by Conventions in three fourths thereof, as the one or the other Mode of Ratification may be proposed by the Congress; Provided that no Amendment which may be made prior to the Year One thousand eight hundred and eight shall in any Manner affect the first and fourth Clauses in the Ninth Section of the first Article; and that no State, without its Consent, shall be deprived of its equal Suffrage in the Senate.

Article. VI.

All Debts contracted and Engagements entered into, before the Adoption of this Constitution, shall be as valid against the United States under this Constitution, as under the Confederation.

This Constitution, and the Laws of the United States which shall be made in Pursuance thereof; and all Treaties made, or which shall be made, under the Authority of the United States, shall be the supreme Law of the Land; and the Judges in every State shall be bound thereby, any Thing in the Constitution or Laws of any State to the Contrary notwithstanding.

The Senators and Representatives before mentioned, and the Members of the several State Legislatures, and all executive and judicial Officers, both of the United States and of the several States, shall be bound by Oath or Affirmation, to support this Constitution; but no religious Test shall ever be required as a Qualification to any Office or public Trust under the United States.

Article. VII.

The Ratification of the Conventions of nine States, shall be sufficient for the Establishment of this Constitution between the States so ratifying the Same.

The Word, "the," being interlined between the seventh and eighth Lines of the first Page, The Word "Thirty" being partly written on an Erazure in the fifteenth Line of the first Page, The Words "is tried" being interlined between the thirty second and thirty third Lines of the first Page and the Word "the" being interlined between the forty third and forty fourth Lines of the second Page.

Attest William Jackson Secretary

done in Convention by the Unanimous Consent of the States present the Seventeenth Day of September in the Year of our Lord one thousand seven hundred and Eighty seven and of the Independance of the United States of America the Twelfth In witness whereof We have hereunto subscribed our Names,

G°. Washington
Presidt and deputy from Virginia

Delaware
Geo. Read
Gunning Bedford jun
John Dickinson
Richard Bassett
Jaco. Broom

Maryland
James McHenry
Dan of St Thos. Jenifer
Danl. Carroll

Virginia
John Blair
James Madison Jr.

North Carolina
Wm. Blount
Richd. Dobbs Spaight
Hu Williamson

South Carolina
J. Rutledge
Charles Cotesworth Pinckney
Charles Pinckney
Pierce Butler

Georgia
William Few
Abr Baldwin

New Hampshire
John Langdon
Nicholas Gilman

Massachusetts
Nathaniel Gorham
Rufus King

Connecticut
Wm. Saml. Johnson
Roger Sherman

New York
Alexander Hamilton

New Jersey
Wil: Livingston
David Brearley
Wm. Paterson
Jona: Dayton

Pennsylvania
B Franklin
Thomas Mifflin
Robt. Morris
Geo. Clymer
Thos. FitzSimons
Jared Ingersoll
James Wilson
Gouv Morris

VOICES OF OUR REPUBLIC

JOHN ADAMS

FOUNDING FATHER

SECOND PRESIDENT OF THE UNITED STATES

Cities may be rebuilt, and a People reduced to Poverty, may acquire fresh Property: But a Constitution of Government once changed from Freedom, can never be restored. Liberty once lost is lost forever. When the People once surrender their share in the Legislature, and their Right of defending the Limitations upon the Government, and of resisting every Encroachment upon them, they can never regain it.

John Adams
John Trumbull
c. 1793
Oil on canvas
National Portrait Gallery, Smithsonian Institution

GLORIA ALLRED

WOMEN'S RIGHTS AND MINORITY RIGHTS ATTORNEY

The preamble to the United States Constitution begins by stating "We the People of the United States, in Order to form a more perfect Union, establish Justice . . . do ordain and establish this Constitution for the United States of America." The US Constitution is an important document, but it does not establish justice for the majority of the American people who are women. In order for there to be equal justice for women under the law we need the addition of the Equal Rights Amendment (ERA) to the United States Constitution, which would simply state "Equality of rights under the law shall not be denied or abridged by the United States or by any State on account of sex." The addition of the ERA would establish a more perfect union and guarantee women and girls equal rights and equal protection under the law.

Photo courtesy of Gloria Allred

DAVID ASMAN

HOST OF FOX BUSINESS NETWORK'S *BULLS & BEARS*

"Free to choose" is the eloquent phrase, immortalized by my mentor and friend Milton Friedman, that describes the essence of what we cherish as a nation. It is embodied in our Constitution, and indeed enshrined by God Himself in his precious gift of free will. It should be our unrelenting guide in constructing or refining the rules and laws by which we are governed. Whatever we do that eases our freedom to choose should be encouraged; and whatever rule denies or restricts that basic wellspring of human life should be avoided. Those three simple words are the hallmark of our freedom and the North Star of its retention.

Photo courtesy of David Asman

RUTH BADER GINSBURG

ASSOCIATE JUSTICE, UNITED STATES SUPREME COURT

Although the word "equal" or "equality" in relation to individual rights does not appear in the original US Constitution or in the first ten amendments that compose the Bill of Rights, the equal dignity of individuals' ideal is part of our constitutional legacy, even of the pre–Civil War original understanding, in this vital sense. The founding fathers rebelled against the patriarchal power of kings and the idea that political authority may legitimately rest on birth status. Their culture held them back from fully perceiving or acting upon ideals of human liberty, equality, and dignity. Thomas Jefferson, for example, when President, told his Secretary of the Treasury: "The appointment of a woman to [public] office is an innovation for which the public is not prepared, nor am I." But the founders stated a commitment in the Declaration of Independence to equality and in the Declaration and the Bill of Rights to individual liberty. Those commitments had growth potential. As historian Richard Morris has written, a prime portion of the history of the US Constitution is the story of the extension (through amendment, judicial interpretation, and practice) of constitutional rights and protections to once-excluded groups: to people once held in bondage, to men without property, to Native Americans, and to women.

Opposite: Collection of the Supreme Court of the United States.

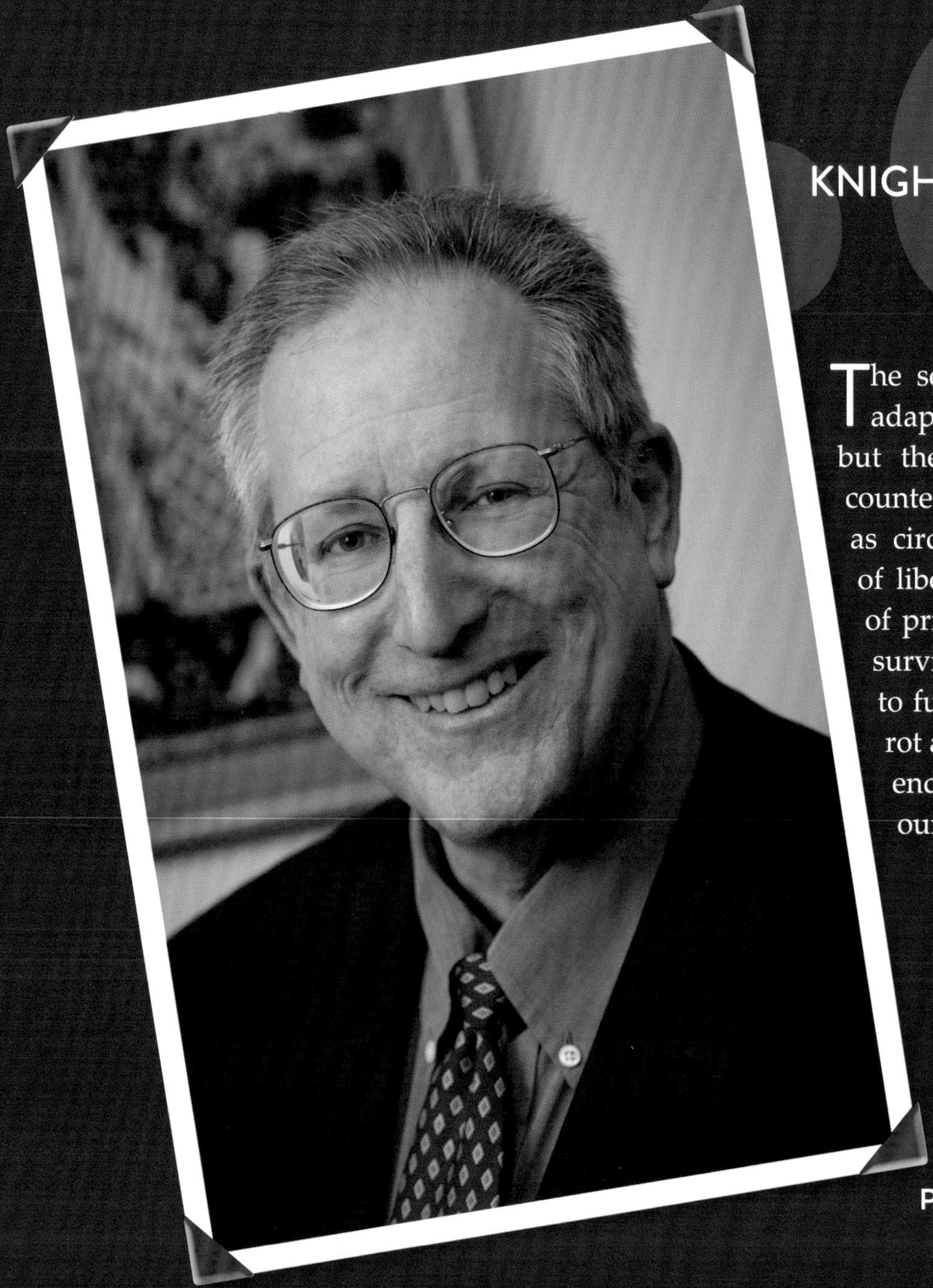

JACK BALKIN

KNIGHT PROFESSOR OF CONSTITUTIONAL LAW AND THE FIRST AMENDMENT

YALE LAW SCHOOL

The secret to our Constitution's success has been its remarkable adaptability to change. Our Constitution has plenty of rules, but their genius is not simple prohibition: Instead, they create countervailing centers of power that can check and balance each other as circumstances change. The Constitution has grand guarantees of liberty and equality, but they are phrased in broad statements of principle that must be worked out over time. The Constitution survives because it is never finished. Each generation has the duty to fulfill its great promises. Without adaptation, our republic will rot and die; that is why the work of constitutional reform is never-ending. The day that the Constitution is finished is the day that our country is finished.

Photo courtesy of Yale University

RANDY E. BARNETT

CARMACK WATERHOUSE PROFESSOR OF LEGAL THEORY

GEORGETOWN UNIVERSITY LAW CENTER

The Constitution secures the rights retained by the People by providing the law that governs those who govern us.

Photo courtesy of Randy Barnett

LOUIS BLACK

CO-FOUNDER
SXSW FESTIVAL & *THE AUSTIN CHRONICLE*

A Constitutional Republic Is an Ugly, Difficult, Frustrating Form of Government.

The current hostile and harsh tone of political discussion has been around since long before the current administration. The only area of general agreement is the government's failure, with a very broad range of attacks on it—specific complaints, accusations, insults, and criticisms—usually determined as much by individual voters' ideology, religion, and philosophy. Ironically, this consensus strongly suggests that the Constitution of the United States is not only working but doing so as intended. The Framers, themselves deeply divided over almost every issue, had no expectation of agreement among the population, but instead expected sharp debate over policies and philosophies. In order to accommodate universal suffrage, they designed the government in such a way as to make getting legislation passed difficult, awkward, and slow-moving—concerned much more that a temporary whim of the majority might have out of proportion consequences than any ease of governing. Instead of articulating focused ideas, championing laws, or detailing the implementation of certain strict beliefs, the document they crafted was about process—laying out a brilliant, flexible, and inclusive government structure, one specifically designed to work amidst public conflict, disagreement, and controversy. Universal suffrage, which seemed to offer empowerment and thus political control to each voter, instead was spread among a population so large and diverse that it almost guaranteed that an individual's input would be very limited. Consequently, citizens disliking certain laws and legislation were frustrated and angry, certain that they were the result of corruption and manipulation. The more widespread the discontent across the whole population the more certain that though perceived as failing, our constitutional government is working as planned.

Photo courtesy of Louis Black

Photo courtesy of Amy Brandwein

AMY BRANDWEIN

OWNER/CHEF, CENTROLINA
AWARD-WINNING RESTAURANT AND MARKET

During my lifetime, I have never witnessed a more important time to cherish the principles in our Constitution and to protect our civil liberties. The First Amendment is currently under daily assault—the right of any citizen to freely comment on policy, the right of a free press free from government censorship, and the right of citizens to assemble to express their viewpoints. Public expression and discourse are key to any democracy and should be protected at all costs. Without it, we have a dictatorship.

STEPHEN BREYER

ASSOCIATE JUSTICE, UNITED STATES SUPREME COURT

Day after day I see before me Americans of every race, religion, nationality, and point of view, trying to resolve their differences, not through war, but in a courtroom—under our Constitution. The Constitution is a brilliant document. Written and adopted in 1787 to 1789, its seven articles and twenty-seven amendments provide a framework for democratic government. It creates a federal government of delegated powers (leaving the rest to the States). It allocates powers among three branches: Legislative, Executive, and Judicial, so that no single group can become too powerful. It requires laws that treat all persons equally. It protects basic individual liberties, such as free speech, free press, free religion, freedom from unreasonable governmental searches and seizures, and fair procedures for those accused of crimes. It helps to guarantee a rule of law.

But its most important characteristic is not written down. A written document is no stronger than the determination of a people to apply and to follow it. President Jackson refused to accept a Supreme Court decision protecting the Cherokee Indians. President Eisenhower sent 1,000 paratroopers to help integrate Little Rock's Central High School. We fought a Civil War to end slavery. We endured eighty years of unlawful racial segregation. Over time, most Americans realized that it is their determination to follow the Constitution, even when doing so is not popular, that lies at the heart of our existence as a free nation under a rule of law.

Today's greatest challenge, necessary to maintain our Constitution, is to encourage younger Americans to learn what the Constitution says, to understand the importance of the rule of law it embodies, and to decide to participate in a democratic public life consistent with the principles that it enunciates. Without that determination, as Benjamin Franklin pointed out many years ago, our Constitution cannot last.

I recommend, as a beginning, that you read it.

Collection of the Supreme Court of the United States

CHRISTOPHER BUCKLEY

NOVELIST; ESSAYIST; HUMORIST; CRITIC; MAGAZINE EDITOR; MEMOIRIST

Tempted as one might be during these, er, interesting times to cite the Twenty-fifth Amendment (the one about replacing presidents), let me instead go with the first three words of our Constitution: *We the people*. What a magnificent nutshell the framers chose with those few simple words, which, read aloud, never fail to raise the hairs on my arm. We're all in this together. To the extent we bear that in mind, how much better off we—and our beloved country—would be.

Photo courtesy of Christopher Buckley

RON CHERNOW

AWARD-WINNING AUTHOR

We tend to think of the US Constitution as chiseled in stone or handed down to us by Roman sages in togas who were writing for the ages. But Washington, Hamilton, and other founders noted that future generations would invariably find imperfections in the document and stressed that it contained language for creating amendments that would rectify any such defects. This feature makes it a living document.

Photo courtesy of Ron Chernow

BOB CHITESTER

FOUNDER/CHAIRMAN
FREE TO CHOOSE NETWORK

In writing the US Constitution, the Founders succeeded in establishing a governing structure that ensures extreme viewpoints are moderated by a process of compromise and consensus without which a free society cannot long exist. They purposely made it difficult to enact new laws; ensured states as well as individuals are represented in the government, thus reconciling urban and rural cultures; and ensured amendments to the Constitution survive the test of rigorous debate. As Milton Friedman wrote, "The ideal is unanimity among responsible individuals achieved on the basis of free and full discussion." We must agree that none of us can have the precise government we think is best. In a free society there are millions of different ideas as to what is best that must be constantly reconciled.

Photo courtesy of
Free To Choose Network

ROGER CLEMENS

BASEBALL LEGEND

Hi, this is the "Rocket" Roger Clemens. I love history, and fortunately over my twenty-four years in the major leagues I was able to make some.

For me, the most profound element of our Constitution is the freedom of speech—a liberty I feel our country not only takes for granted, but also takes advantage of.

Our founding fathers Washington, Hamilton, Adams, Franklin, Madison, and Jefferson (Jefferson, as we know, also wrote the Declaration of Independence) were visionary. These men molded the United States Constitution on the basic rights to free speech and free religion. Most everything else fell into place from those two principles. The freedom to speak without fear of persecution from our government is powerful and should be handled with care.

I personally like free speech when it's innovative and new ideas are formed for the better and common purpose. Bottom line is we're all citizens of this great nation and we want the same fundamental rights:

The opportunity to pursue our interests and advance our talents. To feel safe in our community and country. And to provide for our families and secure our children's futures.

Thank you, and GO USA!

Photo courtesy of Roger Clemens

Photo by Kye Horton, Burning Man Project

KIM COOK

DIRECTOR, ART & CIVIC ENGAGEMENT
BURNING MAN PROJECT

We the People," and the inherent sense of meaning that comes with the word "we," inspires me. It tells me that we are a WE, a union, a collective, a group gathered together for the common good. While my imagination is ignited by the idea of a grand we, I recognize that the "we" refers to an incomplete sense of who belongs. Women and people of color were not included in that we, and gaining the right to vote has not eradicated the disequilibrium established at the time of our founding. We founded a nation based on the genocide of the native inhabitants, and the structural racism and pervasive sexism of our culture has its roots in that founding. I would like to see the Constitution as fluid enough to support change such as adding an equal rights amendment and solid enough to maintain adherence to the Fifteenth Amendment allowing all to vote who are citizens. Can it protect freedom of expression in the First Amendment, while being open enough to revisit the Thirteenth Amendment and not allow slavery even as punishment for a crime—forcing us to look at our incarceration system as an unjust manifestation of that amendment? For me, the Constitution as a foundational document does make possible the United States of America; and I am very clear that there are rights, privileges, and possibilities conveyed by citizenship and supported by the Constitution of which I am a beneficiary. It is my hope that we can look at it, and at our reality, through the lens of the aspirations of the preamble, that we have domestic tranquility, that we promote the general welfare, that we are able to secure the blessings of liberty for those who reside here, and that we are always vigilant that the protections it offers inures to all.

SANDRA DAY O'CONNOR

ASSOCIATE JUSTICE (RETIRED), UNITED STATES SUPREME COURT

Apparently, a great many people have forgotten that the framers of our Constitution went to such great effort to create an independent judicial branch that would not be subject to retaliation by either the executive branch or the legislative branch because of some decision made by those judges.

Photo by Leigh Vogel/
Getty Images for Colonial Williamsburg

ALAN M. DERSHOWITZ

EMERITUS PROFESSOR AT HARVARD LAW SCHOOL

The unique brilliance of our Constitution lies not so much in its substantive provisions, but rather in its structural innovations: namely its federalism, which allocates different powers to the federal and state governments; its separation of powers within the federal government, creating three coequal and separate branches; and its complex system of checks and balances, assuring that no branch may assume unchecked powers. It was not a prescription for efficiency. Instead it was calculated to slow down the exercise of power to protect against tyranny, including the tyranny of temporary majorities. It is, thus, not a document of pure democracy. To be sure, the people—at least the white male people who counted back then—ultimately rule through the ballot box, but they rule through complex structures. The town hall was not the model. That would be too democratic. They were creating a republic. It may seem ironic that the same founders who wrote and signed the radical and lawless Declaration of Independence also wrote and signed so conservative a Constitution just a few years later. But that was to be expected. Revolutionaries require a lawless radical approach relying on natural law and God, because they cannot rely on the written positive law. Nation builders need to create structures that make it difficult for new revolutionaries (such as those who tried to secede in 1860) to do to the new Republic what the colonists did to Great Britain. Hence the difference between our two great documents of liberty. The Declaration was written to justify a treasonous revolution that had already begun and would soon be over. The Constitution—which its critics called "godless"—was written for the ages and has endured longer than any constitution in history, with only a relatively small number of amendments. Despite its many compromises and imperfections, it is one of the most important documents in the history of humankind.

Photo courtesy of Alan M. Dershowitz

JOSÉ DIAZ-BALART

ANCHOR

NOTICIAS TELEMUNDO/NBC *NIGHTLY NEWS SATURDAY*

Photo courtesy of Telemundo

The US Constitution is awe-inspiring. I don't know of any other text in the history of the world that better defines the essence of a nation. It's been more than 200 years since its signing, and yet it is as relevant and current today as it was in 1787.

Even though Thomas Jefferson was not part of the constitutional convention, since he was in France, James Madison made sure that essential parts of Jefferson's concept of democracy were incorporated. One such concept, which Jefferson made clear in his first inaugural address in 1801, rings true in the Constitution: Rule by the majority does not make a democracy. Respect for the minority is just as essential. When either is lost, democracy is imperiled. The US Constitution is extremely concerned about protecting the minority—often, the unpopular minority.

Through the amendment process and the interpretation of the courts, the US Constitution has been preserved, protected, and improved. My profession has been shaped by it. Without the First Amendment, there would be no *Noticias Telemundo* or NBC News. My parents were forced to leave a country where freedom of expression does not exist. The Constitution stands as a shield that guarantees precious and fundamental freedoms. It is extraordinary.

GEN. ANN DUNWOODY, USA, RETIRED

Many Americans don't realize that volunteers for the United States military first raise their right hand and swear to support and defend the Constitution of the United States. I so swore that oath eleven times in the course of my service in the United States Army, pretty heady stuff for a young eighteen-year-old enlistee or anyone else for that matter.

Opposite: Photo courtesy of Ann Dunwoody

JOSEPH J. ELLIS

AWARD-WINNING AUTHOR; HISTORIAN

You can make a case, and Abraham Lincoln did, that America is founded on a proposition, and Thomas Jefferson wrote it. Or you can make a different case that America was founded on an argument about government, and the Constitution provided the framework for its ongoing relevance and resonance.

Photo courtesy of Joseph Ellis

GREGORY L. FENVES

PRESIDENT
UNIVERSITY OF TEXAS

The United States has produced some of the greatest thinkers in history—and this is not a coincidence. It is a consequence of our Constitution. The First Amendment of the US Constitution ensures the rights to freedom of speech, the press, and assembly. Such freedom is essential to inquiry, creative expression, and scientific discovery. These result from the power to question, to critique, and to dream. To embrace new ideas, a society must be prepared to challenge the old ones. And over hundreds of years, our nation has continuously evolved, struggled, and transformed itself to realize the goal of liberty.

As a professor, a university president, and an American, I have seen, firsthand, the genius of our nation's founding document in our universities. The Constitution is anchored in its principles to protect the spark of creativity that lives within the people of a truly free society.

Photo courtesy of Gregory L. Fenves

PHOEBE FERGUSON

EXECUTIVE DIRECTOR/CO-FOUNDER
THE PLESSY AND FERGUSON FOUNDATION

When I think about all of the current efforts to undo the progress made during and after the civil rights movement, it is easy to feel overwhelmed with despair. This quote from the Talmud helps me move forward every day to do my part to advance the cause of equity and justice mandated in our Constitution:

"Do not be daunted by the enormity of the world's grief. Do justly now, love mercy now, walk humbly now. You are not obligated to complete the work, but neither are you free to abandon it."

Photo courtesy of Phoebe Ferguson

STEVE FORBES

CHAIRMAN AND EDITOR-IN-CHIEF, FORBES MEDIA

The High Court, with occasional exceptions, has deferred more and more to the other two branches of government when they've committed acts that violate the basic law of the land, especially if the laws have expanded the power of the government. Liberal justices long ago adopted the attitude that the president should pretty much be free to do as he wishes if he's advancing modern liberalism. Our Founders focused on how laws are enacted. Today the focus is on the ends, not the means, which, of course, leads to tyranny.

Photo courtesy of Steve Forbes

RALPH FRIEDMAN

RET. NYPD DETECTIVE

Photo courtesy of Ralph Friedman

To me, the United States Constitution represents what America is and stands for. As a retired NYPD detective, I was sworn in to uphold the Constitution of the United States (2/2/70). It's the foundation of our country's laws and rights that all police officers risk their lives every day to protect. At the time of its signing, it brought our fledging country together, strengthened our government, and introduced basic rights to all citizens that myself and all law enforcement wholeheartedly believe in and protect. It's sad that some people today don't appreciate how precious these rights are and how well it protects them and gives them the rights and freedoms they have...

NEIL GORSUCH

ASSOCIATE JUSTICE, UNITED STATES SUPREME COURT

Ours is the job of interpreting the Constitution. And that document isn't some inkblot on which litigants may project their hopes and dreams for a new and perfected tort law, but a carefully drafted text judges are charged with applying according to its original public meaning. If a party wishes to claim a constitutional right, it is incumbent on him to tell us where it lies, not to assume or stipulate with the other side that it must be in there someplace.

Opposite: Collection of the Supreme Court of the United States

DAVE GRANLUND

CARTOONIST AND ILLUSTRATOR

Photo courtesy of Dave Granlund

Celebrating the First Amendment...
SPEECH
PRESS
RELIGION
ASSEMBLY
PETITION
Freedoms
DAVE GRANLUND © www.davegranlund.com

MICHAEL GREVE

PROFESSOR, ANTONIN SCALIA LAW SCHOOL
GEORGE MASON UNIVERSITY

Photo courtesy of George Mason University

The Constitution's most unique feature, shared by no other country, is its omnipresence in our public, political, and intellectual debate. The Framers *intended* that remarkable result. The Constitution eschews both legalese and gaseous aspirations; it is written so that ordinary citizens can engage and debate it. And through the separation of powers and federalism, the Constitution invites rival institutional claims to represent the actual sovereign: We the People. Because every such claim will be both interested and contestable, there can never be a Constitution above all politics, accessible only to a guardian elite of lawyers. And by inviting political actors to claim contestable constitutional ground, the Constitution itself constitutionalizes our ordinary politics.

Something close to this is what Chief Justice John Marshall called "the genius of our institutions." That strikes me as right; and it's not a bad way of running a free country.

ALEXANDER HAMILTON

FOUNDING FATHER

The truth is, after all the declamations we have heard, that the Constitution is itself, in every rational sense, and to every useful purpose, A BILL OF RIGHTS.

ANDREW HAMILTON, PHD, FRS

PRESIDENT, NEW YORK UNIVERSITY

Photo courtesy of Kate Lord/New York University

As a Briton who made his way to these shores thirty-seven years ago and was won over by the American experiment, I feel a certain kinship towards the original authors of the Constitution of the United States. I would not be so bold as to claim peerage with their brilliance—all the more astonishing when you consider their relative youth—but like them I saw the attraction in starting over and dreaming big in a new country.

My training as a scientist gives me a particular appreciation for the simplicity, brevity, and precision of the document and its language. Specifically in these uncertain times, we Americans continue to owe the framers a debt of gratitude. Though the Constitution was inspired greatly by British case law, the British "constitution" remains implied, and subject to interpretation and ultimately the fidelity of leaders and institutions. Here in the US, the founders took a more skeptical view of human nature and assuming "men were not angels" constructed a system of checks and balances that has moored us even through the most tumultuous of political waters.

AMY HANIFAN

OPERATIONS CHIEF, McMINNVILLE FIRE DEPARTMENT

The Nineteenth Amendment was truly one of the greatest steps towards achieving equity for women. I am forever indebted to those who worked so hard towards that goal, which still holds an important place today.

Photo courtesy of Amy Hanifan

SUSAN HERMAN

PRESIDENT, AMERICAN CIVIL LIBERTIES UNION
CENTENNIAL PROFESSOR OF LAW, BROOKLYN LAW SCHOOL

The Constitution commits us to respecting fundamental principles—like freedom of speech, due process, and equal protection—regardless of our individual liberal or conservative points of view.

Federalists and Anti-Federalists who disagreed about almost everything else nevertheless managed to agree on the terms of the Constitution because they knew that we would need neutral principles to govern our politics. Those principles should still serve as a beacon in our own hyper-partisan age.

Photo courtesy of Susan Herman

Photo courtesy of James C. Ho

JAMES C. HO

JUDGE, UNITED STATES COURT OF APPEALS FOR THE FIFTH CIRCUIT

Our Founders loved freedom and feared government power. Driven by these principles, they waged a revolution—and then wrote a Constitution. Because of their bravery, a new country was born. Because of their genius, our written Constitution endures.

Their genius was not just in putting our liberties into writing. It was in entrusting our liberties to a particular form of government—a structure of government that diffuses power horizontally across three rival branches, and vertically between federal and state authorities. Separating power to limit power. Harnessing ambition to counteract ambition. All to make it difficult for the government to gang up on the citizen.

Lawmaking in the hands of the most politically accountable. Law enforcement in separate hands to avoid mob rule. And government subject to review by a judiciary independent of the other two. A structure that is protective of our liberties—so long as we are faithful to our written Constitution.

Photo courtesy of James C. Ho

LYNNE JACKSON

PRESIDENT, DRED SCOTT HERITAGE FOUNDATION

GREAT-GREAT-GRANDDAUGHTER OF DRED AND HARRIET SCOTT

Photo courtesy of Lynne Jackson

In the opinion of most, the Constitution was misinterpreted in the *Dred Scott* decision of 1857. That interpretation condemned a whole race of people to forever be property and not citizens by superseding the heart of the Declaration of Independence with the Fifth Amendment. But for the outcome of the Civil War, those fates may have been sealed.

The Constitution self-corrected with the Thirteenth, Fourteenth, and Fifteenth Amendments to undo the misappropriation that many of the Founders in their compromising condition never intended.

President James Madison is considered the Father of the Constitution. I chose to stand next to him on my first visit to Statuary Hall in Philadelphia. (My maiden name is also Madison.) It seemed appropriate to "meet" the man who set the tone for that document which, via *Dred Scott*, no longer denied the rights of freedom and citizenship for the underclass. Benjamin Franklin's indirect comments on the document, "A Republic, if you can keep it," means more today than ever.

THOMAS JEFFERSON

FOUNDING FATHER; THIRD PRESIDENT OF THE UNITED STATES

I had rather ask an enlargement of power from the nation, where it is found necessary, than to assume it by a construction which would make our powers boundless. Our peculiar security is in the possession of a written Constitution. Let us not make it a blank paper by construction.

ANDY JOBSON

ENGLISH DEPARTMENT CHAIR
RIVERSIDE MILITARY ACADEMY

I'm grateful to Lin-Manuel Miranda (*Hamilton*) for sparking interest in my children for the times and trials of our Framers. However, interest isn't the same as understanding. When I asked my teenager what she really knew about the Constitution, she told me a little about the *Federalist Papers*, but didn't know much about what was in the document itself.

I don't fault Mr. Miranda; Hamilton had a full life, and I'm not surprised that the details of the document he so strongly defended didn't get into the musical. However, in a world in which compromise is increasingly rare, I want our youth to study the convention and the document it produced.

Our government is messy; we often get frustrated at the slow rate of change when we see something that needs fixing. At the same time, the genius of the plan that laboriously emerged from those hot weeks in 1787 is that it does everything possible to give every group, every person, a defense against those who see the world differently. I doubt a single signer of the original document liked everything in it, but each recognized the merits contained therein, and believed in the ability of future generations to wrestle with their own problems. Students today can greatly benefit from this lesson in compromise.

Photo courtesy of Andy Jobson

EDITH H. JONES

JUDGE, UNITED STATES COURT OF APPEALS FOR THE FIFTH CIRCUIT

The United States Constitution is great because, for over two hundred tumultuous years, it has preserved ordered liberty under limited government for We the People. We must not forget Justice Joseph Story's comment about this framework in the preface to his *Commentaries on the Constitution*:

> "Upon subjects of government it has always appeared to me, that metaphysical refinements are out of place. A constitution of government is addressed to the common sense of the people; and never was designed for trials of logical skill, or visionary speculation."

Two principles follow from this insight. First, because the Constitution presupposes that citizens with common sense can perform the challenging task of self-government, civic and moral education are a never-ending duty. Second, citizens must recognize the risk in entrusting government to "experts." The tendency of logicians and visionaries is to attempt perfection, often at the expense of simplicity, common sense, and even liberty. The Constitution preserves liberty under law not only by balancing competing political passions, but by establishing a government "simple" enough to be understood by and accountable to the People.

Photo courtesy of Edith Jones

MOJ ↑
CCCI ←
المحكمة المركزية

JACKIE JOYNER-KERSEE

FIVE-TIME OLYMPIC MEDALIST

Perhaps I most appreciate the US Constitution's Bill of Rights protecting individual liberty and justice while placing restrictions on the powers of government. As an active philanthropist in children's education, racial equality, and women's rights, I have felt the profound impact of the first ten amendments on my life.

Photo courtesy of Jackie Joyner-Kersee

Photo courtesy of Jonathan Karl

JONATHAN KARL

CHIEF WHITE HOUSE CORRESPONDENT
ABC NEWS

Freedom of speech and freedom of the press are included in the very first amendment to the Constitution for good reason. Without the freedom to question, criticize, and hold accountable those in power, the other freedoms guaranteed by the Constitution could not long endure.

VIRGINIA KASE

CHIEF EXECUTIVE OFFICER
LEAGUE OF WOMEN VOTERS

In 1920 women won the right to vote—but not all women were equally able to exercise that right because of their race. Moving into the next 100 years, I want to ensure no woman is ever again denied the right to participate in our democracy as full and equal citizens. I think of all the women who fought tirelessly and suffered great indignation for the right to vote, and I want to honor their legacy. I think of future generations of women whose voting rights we are fighting for today and I don't want to let them down. That is why at the League of Women Voters, we fight for equality at the ballot box so that in our democracy, every American woman can own her power and make her voice heard.

Photo courtesy of League of Women Voters

BRETT M. KAVANAUGH

ASSOCIATE JUSTICE, UNITED STATES SUPREME COURT

In its design and structure, the Constitution tilts toward liberty. To protect individual liberty, the Framers separated the power to legislate from the power to enforce from the power to adjudicate. The Framers made it difficult to enact legislation, requiring action by the House, the Senate, and the President. The Framers then created a separate Executive who independently enforces the law and who can exercise prosecutorial discretion and the pardon power to further protect individual liberty. And the Framers established an independent Judiciary that has the power (with a jury) to determine whether an individual has in fact violated the law as alleged by the Executive and whether the law in question is consistent with the Constitution. Before the coercive power of the Federal Government may act upon a citizen, the Constitution imposes many barriers. Why? To protect individual liberty. Structure protects liberty.

Opposite: Collection of the Supreme Court of the United States

TED KOPPEL

ANCHOR & MANAGING EDITOR OF *NIGHTLINE* (1980-2005)
SENIOR CONTRIBUTOR, *CBS SUNDAY MORNING*

The value of the Constitution lies in its ability to withstand close and endless examination and in the wisdom of its authors who anticipated the need for rare but essential amendments. Without diminishing for a moment the content of the document, consider the media used in its drafting: parchment, quill and ink; a combination designed neither for speed nor immediate and widespread dissemination. We, on the other hand, have achieved a greater capacity to communicate more, further and faster than ever before. Rather than using information to illuminate the world, though, we consume it like fuel. The more we burn, the faster we go. The faster we go, the less we see and understand. We slow down only for the accidents along the side of the road; and the biggest accident still lies ahead. Only, I fear, when that occurs—only when the human and social costs of treating truth and lies like fungible commodities leave us wondering where and why we lost our footing as a nation—will we come to realize that WHAT is communicated to us is vastly more important than the medium by which it is conveyed. Some are already posing the question; but one day, most Americans will point at us in the news media and say: "Why didn't you tell us? Why did you encourage all that bile and venom? Why did you feed us all that trivial crap, when so many terrible things were converging?" And no one will be happy with the answer. Least of all, those of us who offer it. "What we gave you," we will say, "is what you wanted." That is when the Constitution will be put to its greatest test.

Photo courtesy of Ted Koppel

ALAN CHARLES KORS

HENRY CHARLES LEA PROFESSOR EMERITUS OF HISTORY
UNIVERSITY OF PENNSYLVANIA

The promise of our Republic, as expression of the Lockean tradition, as reflection of the Enlightenment, and in part perhaps (I always hoped) as entreaty to the future, shone from our founding Declaration of Independence: legal equality in the enjoyment of unalienable rights. The amendments we should cherish have brought more and more citizens into the historically precious achievement of that status. None honored and helped fulfill that promise more than the Fourteenth Amendment, in a concise statement of the equal justice toward which the United States, in fits and starts, has steadily moved: "No State shall make or enforce any law which shall . . . deny to any person within its jurisdiction the equal protection of the laws." The Amendment, aided by incorporation and the golden phrase, "any person within its jurisdiction," unleashed a dynamic toward that legal equality which is the ongoing political and moral mission, and splendor, of America.

Photo courtesy of Alan Charles Kors

PHIL LABONTE

MUSICIAN
ALL THAT REMAINS

It's frequently argued whether or not the Constitution is a "living, breathing document," though the very reason the Constitution is written down is precisely because it is not alive. The Founders had enough foresight not to design a constitution that could be creatively reinterpreted and changed at a whim by our government.

This is in direct contrast to the system of jurisprudence our young nation had just fought a war to escape. The powers granted to government by our Constitution, and the specific rights protected in the Bill of Rights, are not transient. The Founders' intent was for our government to be as small as possible while still possessing the authority and power to protect the rights of its citizens.

If the Constitution were intended to be transient, with its meaning changing with the times (and the opinion of each new government elected), there would be little point in having a written Constitution at all. In fact, it would render our Constitution all but useless.

I would even go further with this line of argument—if the Founding Fathers had intended the Constitution to be changed with the whims of every new elected Congress, why would there be an amendment process contained in the document at all? And why would the amendment process be so stringent?

The demandingness of the amendment process itself is the strongest argument against a living Constitution one can make, and this is not something that should be viewed negatively. The Constitution protects us from the whims of imperfect human beings, and only because of that it protects the inalienable rights of all the people. This is something we should celebrate and most jealously protect from those who would work to weaken or circumvent the limits enshrined within what is a unique document that empowers the whole of the people.

Photo courtesy of Roxy Faith Alexandria

JO ANN LEACH

TEACHER
KANSAS CITY PUBLIC SCHOOL DISTRICT

Photo courtesy of Molly Uhlenhake

I am a sixty-four-year-old wife and mother of two grown daughters. My generation saw the fabric of the Constitution pulled and stretched but never torn. My father served in World War II, and my brother served in Vietnam. I was nine when the Civil Rights Act was passed and seventeen when Title IX was enacted and *Roe v. Wade* was decided. I went from law school to the state public defender's office, where I represented people who committed unspeakable crimes, were despised for it, and faced the ultimate penalty, but who always received fair and full due process of law. Today, I am a Montessori teacher in a public school with twenty to twenty-five three- to six-year-olds in my class each year. These children come from widely disparate ethnic, social, and economic backgrounds. They have extremely different aptitudes, abilities, opportunities, impediments, and challenges. I worry for all of them—for some because I know how hard their lives are likely to be, but for each because I want their potential to be given every chance. When I look at these children through the eyes of my experience, I am counting on the enduring truths of our Constitution to guide our country in their time. I trust us as a people to ensure that it will.

SETH LIPSKY

EDITOR

THE NEW YORK SUN

The Constitution is a unifying document. It requires that our officers, judges, and legislators, both of the United States and the several States, be bound by oath to support not king or country but rather the Constitution itself. Then comes its most emphatic sentence: But no religious test shall ever be required as a qualification to any office or public trust under the United States. No. Ever. Any.

JAMES MADISON

FOUNDING FATHER; FOURTH PRESIDENT OF THE UNITED STATES

As a guide in expounding and applying the provisions of the Constitution, the debates and incidental decisions of the Convention can have no authoritative character. However desirable it be that they should be preserved as a gratification to the laudable curiosity felt by every people to trace the origin and progress of their political Institutions, & as a source perhaps of some lights on the Science of Govt. the legitimate meaning of the Instrument must be derived from the text itself; or if a key is to be sought elsewhere, it must be not in the opinions or intentions of the Body which planned & proposed the Constitution, but in the sense attached to it by the people in their respective State Conventions where it recd. all the authority which it possesses.

LEO MELAMED

CHAIRMAN/CEO, MELAMED & ASSOCIATES, INC.

CHAIRMAN EMERITUS, CME GROUP, INC.

In his book *Free to Choose*, Milton Friedman asserts that the story of the United States is a story of two interdependent miracles: an economic miracle and a political miracle. Each miracle resulted from a separate set of revolutionary ideas—both sets of ideas, by a curious coincidence, were formulated in the same year, 1776.

One set of ideas was embodied in Adam Smith's *The Wealth of Nations*; the second set of ideas, drafted by Thomas Jefferson, was embodied in the Declaration of Independence and the US Constitution.

During the two centuries following their introduction, when these two ideals were applied to a people with an immigrant ancestry, of a multi-cultural heritage, and a multi-racial composition, they produced an unimaginable result. They became a lightning rod for ideas. They created a crucible for innovation. They combined to become the decisive driver of progress in science, technology, and economic development.

Photo courtesy of Leo Melamed

CANDICE MILLARD

AUTHOR

The Constitution is structure. It's stability, freedom, justice, and hope. It strengthens and defines us. Without it, who, as a nation, are we?

Photo courtesy of Candice Millard

JANET NAPOLITANO

PRESIDENT, UNIVERSITY OF CALIFORNIA; FORMER SECRETARY OF HOMELAND SECURITY

US Constitution, First Amendment: "Congress shall make no law respecting an establishment of religion, or prohibiting the free exercise thereof; or abridging the freedom of speech, or of the press; or the right of the people peaceably to assemble, and to petition the Government for a redress of grievances."

Too often students and others have shouted down speakers with whom they disagree, or set out to prevent them from speaking at all. The productive way to deal with extreme, unfounded speech is not with less speech but more—with a vibrant discourse informed by facts and persuasive argument. I prefer a loud campus, where students feel included and encouraged to give voice to different perspectives and where faculty members invite conflicting opinions and enforce their own professional standards. These are the lodestars that should guide efforts to ensure freedom of expression on American campuses.

Photo courtesy of Janet Napolitano

CLARK NEILY

VICE PRESIDENT FOR CRIMINAL JUSTICE
CATO INSTITUTE

The Constitution is a charter of liberty and blueprint for limited government. It is not just a rulebook or an operating manual but an ethos—it is a commitment to the proposition that no individual or institution stands above the law, and no law stands above the fundamental right of every human being to peacefully pursue their own version of the good life. The founders understood that government stands as a perpetual threat to that right, and so they designed the Constitution to serve as its perpetual guardian.

Photo courtesy of Clark Neily

AMELIA A. NEWCOMB

MANAGING EDITOR, *CHRISTIAN SCIENCE MONITOR*

AND

KATE DILLINGHAM

CELLIST; EXECUTIVE DIRECTOR; PRODUCER

GREAT-GREAT-GRANDDAUGHTERS OF JUSTICE JOHN MARSHALL HARLAN

In discussing our great-great-grandfather, Justice John Marshall Harlan, we've tried to imagine the personal consequences of his "lone dissent" in 1896 in *Plessy v. Ferguson*. To quote Frederick Douglass, it must have been a "delicate and difficult" task to be the only Supreme Court justice to stand up for African Americans' civil rights in the social climate of the day. His courage and moral conviction are inspiring not only to us but to many, many others as well.

A number of Harlan's experiences in childhood and adulthood may have informed his jurisprudence. He was raised in a slave-owning family in Kentucky. He had a lifelong relationship with Robert Harlan, a half-white, half-black child who was raised in the Harlan household and later became a prominent Ohio citizen and legislator. John Harlan also sustained lasting physical and emotional scars from an unsuccessful attempt to save the life of a young slave girl whose clothing accidentally caught fire. During the Civil War, he raised a militia to fight for the Union Army. But ultimately, the Constitution was his guide. The power of Harlan's stand against the codification of racial segregation was recognized by Douglass. As he wrote supportively to Harlan, "I wish to assure you, if you are alone on the Bench, you are not alone in the country."

Photo courtesy of Northside Independent School District

JACK NICKLAUS

"THE GOLDEN BEAR"
PROFESSIONAL GOLFER

There is a simple reason why I shed a tear every time I hear the national anthem, and that is because of a deep-rooted love for our country and an unwavering respect for all those who centuries ago fought for the rights and freedoms we should cherish today, and those who still fight today for those same rights. There is nothing free about freedom, and there are men and women today sacrificing life and limb to protect those freedoms and the constitutional rights—be it freedom of religion, speech or due process—we all still enjoy today, and perhaps too often take for granted.

Photo courtesy of Jim Mandeville and the Nicklaus Companies

JIM OBERGEFELL

SPEAKER/AUTHOR

Emma Parker Photography

The Fourteenth Amendment of the Constitution is especially important to me because it means my marriage to John Arthur exists in the eyes of the law. As the culmination of the fight many other plaintiffs and I waged, the *Obergefell v. Hodges* Supreme Court decision brought marriage equality to every state of our nation. This decision, rooted in the Fourteenth Amendment, means same-sex couples across our nation can participate in marriage, one of the most meaningful and important human institutions, and legal recognition of those relationships doesn't vary based on state of residence. Personally, this gives me comfort knowing my late husband John can truly Rest In Peace because the state of Ohio can never erase our marriage from his death certificate, and I can legally forever call myself John's widower.

KEITH PLESSY

PRESIDENT/CO-FOUNDER
THE PLESSY AND FERGUSON FOUNDATION
GREAT-GREAT-GRANDSON OF HOMER PLESSY

Shining a light on Thurgood Marshall: He and his team of lawyers never gave up on Homer Plessy's 1896 challenge in *Plessy v. Ferguson*, using the Fourteenth Amendment arguments.

The Fourteenth Amendment's last words shined the light on the decision in *Brown v. Board*, ultimately overturning the *Plessy* decision—

". . . nor deny to any person within its jurisdiction the equal protection of the laws"—my favorite quote from the Fourteenth Amendment.

Photo courtesy of Keith Plessy

JOHN POPPER

MUSICIAN; SONGWRITER
BLUES TRAVELER

Photo courtesy of John Popper

The US Constitution is perhaps the oldest and arguably the finest still extant example of a "living document" that perpetually attempts and reattempts to directly interpret the will of a people consented to be governed by its decree.

Consider the concept of an up-to-date "will of the people" as current as can be made with as true a representation of those people as can be fairly represented.

The mere aspiration for such a document in and of itself is a monumental leap forward for the free will of all humankind, and however imperfectly it is put into practice still keeps alive that aspiration . . . ultimately the precious as yet undying hope that freedom can be more than mere hope for any of us . . . for all of us.

It is in fact a promise, not just to Americans, but to everyone on this earth that there is a place where hope, freedom, and even justice can be redeemed.

PRISCILLA PRESLEY

FOUNDER OF ELVIS PRESLEY ENTERPRISES; ACTRESS; PRODUCER; ANIMAL RIGHTS PHILANTHROPIST

The Nineteenth Amendment of the US Constitution gave women the right to vote 100 years ago. I am grateful to the women who fought for that right and achieved it peacefully. Today, my daughter, granddaughters, and I stand on the shoulders of intelligent, strong, and brave women in order to cast our votes.

Photo courtesy of Priscilla Presley

JONATHAN RAUCH

AUTHOR/JOURNALIST;
SENIOR FELLOW, BROOKINGS INSTITUTION

I have been a First Amendment fanboy since my teens. As a Jew, I instinctively understood that freedom of speech and conscience are the only safe space for minorities. Later, as a journalist, I learned firsthand that the free expression of information and ideas is the lifeblood of a democracy.

Still later, when I realized I was gay, I became an outspoken advocate of same-sex marriage, thanks to the First Amendment. In 1958, in *One, Inc. v Olesen*, the Supreme Court struck down the US Postal Service's ban on ONE, America's first pro-gay magazine. That little-known but seminal decision gave homosexual Americans our voices, and it's the reason I'm married to my husband today.

By the way: the cover article of the issue of *ONE* which the Postmaster General unconstitutionally banned? "You Can't Print It!", a critique of the Postmaster General's censorship practices. Enough said.

Photo courtesy of Jonathan Rauch

ROB RIGGLE

ACTOR; LT. COL. USMC (RET)

I will support and defend the Constitution of the United States against all enemies…

This is how the enlistment oath begins for all members of the United States military. As a Marine, our core values are Honor, Courage, and Commitment. Our motto is Semper Fidelis… Always Faithful. When I took that oath to defend the Constitution, I took those values and that motto to heart. For anyone who pledges life and limb to protect the Constitution, there is a belief in something bigger than themselves. The Constitution guarantees my freedoms. It guarantees my children's freedom. It guarantees millions of Americans in the future, who I'll never know, freedom as well. To those whom came before me, who gave everything so that I could enjoy those freedoms today, there will never be enough gratitude. Other than raising my children, defending the Constitution of the United States is one of my greatest honors in life.

Photo by Sean Hagwell

MARK SCHLISSEL

PRESIDENT
UNIVERSITY OF MICHIGAN

What I respect most about the Constitution is how it balances democracy with the rights of the individual. It protects minority opinion and personal liberty, while at the same time assuring that government actions reflect the democratic will of the people. The Bill of Rights along with more than two centuries of American jurisprudence also protects minority groups from suppression by majority opinion of the day. As an educator and academic leader, I hold the First Amendment most dear. It underlies the academic freedom of our faculty and protects the unfettered discussion and debate needed to make discoveries, achieve new levels of understanding, and cultivate the curiosity and creativity of our students.

Photo courtesy of Mark Schlissel

ARNOLD SCHWARZENEGGER

FORMER GOVERNOR OF CALIFORNIA; ACTOR; FILMMAKER

California State Archive photo by Duncan McIntosh

When I came to the United States, I had nothing but a gym bag and a dream. I was alone, in a new country.

But I had faith in the vision that brought me to America, and that was enough. I knew that this country was the land of opportunity, the launch pad for dreamers like me. The rest is history, and everything I have accomplished, I owe to the United States of America.

What makes the United States such a magnet for the biggest dreams in the world? What inspires the world to come here to accomplish their goals? The simple answer is that we are the home of freedom and equality.

But a home built without a foundation will not stand. Luckily, our founding fathers laid an incredible, lasting foundation: our United States Constitution.

The story of the drafting of our constitution is the story of America. People came together from all different backgrounds to collaborate, debate, and come to agreement. The drafters weren't all best friends—some of them didn't even like each other. Some were bitter political enemies. But when they came together in Philadelphia, they had a common vision: protecting freedom and equality for future generations, and laying a foundation that all future Americans could continue to build on.

We should always remember the vision, the cooperation, the compromise, and the selflessness that produced our founding document. That is the spirit of America, and I love the Constitution because it is a constant reminder of our enduring spirit that brought me to this country.

LEAH WARD SEARS

GEORGIA SUPREME COURT CHIEF JUSTICE (RETIRED); PARTNER, SMITH, GAMBRELL & RUSSELL

Over two hundred years ago a group of wealthy white men wrote the Constitution of the United States. But when they did so, it wasn't their intention that the rights they had decreed would have anything to do with black people or women. In fact, the freedoms, aspirations, and rights of non-white, non-male persons simply weren't considerations in the original document. This grievous omission has long informed, and fueled, most of my life's important decisions, including what I studied in school (law), where I chose to live (Atlanta, Georgia, the cradle of the Civil Rights Movement), and even who I married (an African studies scholar). Why? Because I know that the playing field outlined in the Constitution isn't level yet. Which means that it's often a struggle to be accepted for who I am and what I have to give notwithstanding that I'm also African-American and female. And as long as that's the case, I'm not free. The awareness of this runs deep.

Photo courtesy of Leah Ward Sears

GENE SIMMONS

MUSICIAN; SONGWRITER; PRODUCER; ACTOR
KISS

The Constitution of the United States is the foundation that makes America great. While I was not born in the United States, I am a proud legal immigrant, living the American dream because I was endowed with the same constitutional rights and limitless opportunities as those born here. "We the people" . . . it does not get more powerful than that.

Photo courtesy of Gene Simmons

EVAN SPIEGEL

CO-FOUNDER & CHIEF EXECUTIVE OFFICER
SNAP, INC.

I've always felt that our democratic ideals truly took shape when George Washington left office after two terms. The precedent he set in 1797 has since been solidified in the Twenty-second Amendment that provides term limits for the President of the United States. Establishing term limits reaffirms that our shared vision of freedom, equality, and justice for all transcends individual leadership.

Photo courtesy of Evan Spiegel

BEN STEIN

SPEECHWRITER; ACTOR; LAWYER; ECONOMIST

The genius of the Constitution is that it recognizes that human beings are ambitious, greedy, cruel, not always smart, and that even the most exalted of them can and will try to seek dangerous power over their fellows. The Constitution puts up roadblocks against such people and at the same time organizes their energy to produce immense results in war and peace, a steam locomotive barreling down the track towards a bright tomorrow under ordered freedom.

Photo courtesy of Ben Stein

NADINE STROSSEN

JOHN MARSHALL HARLAN II PROFESSOR OF LAW
NEW YORK LAW SCHOOL

I especially cherish the Preamble's declaration that "We the People . . . establish this Constitution . . . in Order to . . . secure the Blessings of Liberty to ourselves and our Posterity." Although this inspiring language does not impose any specific obligation on government officials, it does lay out core values that should guide them in exercising their powers. Likewise, it should guide the courts' interpretations of the Constitution's many open-textured provisions, such as the ones that guarantee to all "persons" both "due process" and "equal protection."

The Preamble echoes the Declaration of Independence's inherent human rights philosophy that all people "are endowed by their Creator with certain unalienable Rights," and that "Governments are instituted" in order "to secure these rights." Of course, the original Constitution contained provisions that directly violated this core commitment, including by enshrining slavery, and government officials still fall short of actually "secur[ing] . . . Liberty" for all of us. Nonetheless, throughout history we have moved ever closer to that lofty ideal through tools that the Constitution itself provides, including constitutional amendments and enforcement by an independent judiciary.

Photo courtesy of Nadine Strossen

ARTHUR SULZBERGER JR.

CHAIRMAN OF THE BOARD OF THE NEW YORK TIMES COMPANY; FORMER PUBLISHER OF THE *NEW YORK TIMES* (1992-2017)

In the spring of 1971, as my father prepared to publish the Pentagon Papers, the *Times*'s longtime law firm issued a warning: If you go to print, you could be personally hauled to jail, the paper could face financial ruin . . . and we won't defend you.

But my father never wavered. The *Times* pressed on. The lawyers were fired. We released the documents, exposing decades of government deception and wasted carnage. And the Supreme Court affirmed our First Amendment right to do so.

The Constitution empowers the press to seek truth, hold power to account, and expose wrongdoing. And that's what we at the *Times* have done—no matter who, or what, we're up against.

In 2005, bucking presidential pressure, I followed my father's example by revealing the government's illegal wiretapping program. And my son, A.G., went to the Oval Office in 2019 and forcefully told the president of the United States that the press will never be the enemy of the people.

Freedom of the press is what permits fearless journalism, the kind that makes our democracy function—and that makes the world more transparent, more informed, and more just. Our country needs that now more than ever.

Photo courtesy of New York Times

Photo courtesy of Jim Taylor & Barbara Potter

JIM TAYLOR & BARBARA POTTER

DIRECTOR & PRODUCER

A MORE OR LESS PERFECT UNION PBS DOCUMENTARY

While filming *A More or Less Perfect Union* we found that everyone we talked to had an opinion about the US Constitution, but very few had actually read it.

CHUCK TODD

POLITICAL DIRECTOR, NBC NEWS; MODERATOR, *MEET THE PRESS*

There are so many ways I like to describe the Constitution but the one I prefer the most, particularly in my profession as a journalist, is this: the rule book. Discerning the rule book's meaning is at the core of all of our debates, not just the ones we argue about the most, but all of them in our free society. Our elections are about who—in party and in personality and character—we want interpreting this "rule book." So important is this document to me that I carry a pocket version in my suit coat with me every day. It's there because I do believe it's important I refresh myself on certain aspects when preparing to moderate any policy discussion. But there's a symbolic reason as well: every time I take the pocket rule book out of my coat at night or stick it in before I leave in the morning, it's a reminder of both what gives me the freedom to do my job and the burden of responsibility I have in helping to defend it.

Photo courtesy of NBC News

JANINE TURNER

ACTRESS; FOUNDER & CO-PRESIDENT OF CONSTITUTING AMERICA

As I traverse the country speaking with students about the United States Constitution, I inform them that I want them to feel empowered about being a part of the government. The Constitution is their empowerment. The supreme law of the land maintains freedom from tyranny by preserving their unalienable rights, which enables them to hold elected officials accountable. They can utilize such wondrous power by knowing the laws within the Constitution and by knowing how to apply them. If they are confused, *Our Constitution Rocks* by Juliette Turner can assist. I say, "Within the First Amendment are the 'four step tools' to effect change: write a simple petition, use speech to inform others, call the press to spread the word, march with a peaceful assembly. You are never too young to engage. The United States government is not to be a mystery. It is for you and it starts with you."

Photo courtesy of Janine Turner

CATHERINE VALERIO BARRAD

GENERAL COUNSEL
CALIFORNIA STATE UNIVERSITY

What I find most remarkable about the Constitution is how it creates a space in which Americans of widely disparate backgrounds can vehemently disagree but still peacefully coexist. The Constitution's fundamental balance of individual liberty and limited government cannot work without free expression, because a government that controls its people's speech is no longer limited. As Justice Oliver Wendell Holmes said in emphasizing the importance of tolerance for disagreement, "the principle of free thought is not free thought for those who agree with us but freedom for the thought that we hate."

Nowhere is this principle more important than on college campuses, where academic freedom—the freedom to explore and debate the value of all ideas—cannot flourish if only certain speech is allowed. While we may find some of what is said unpalatable or offensive, shutting down speech because we do not agree with it is abdicating our shared responsibility to challenge thought, to engage in civil debate about it, and to evaluate contrary viewpoints on their merits. I see this lively discourse every day on our wonderfully diverse campuses and, in their encouragement of more speech rather than limited speech, I witness our Constitution at work.

Photo courtesy of David Barrad

DENISE DORING VAN BUREN

PRESIDENT GENERAL
NATIONAL SOCIETY DAUGHTERS OF THE AMERICAN REVOLUTION

As American citizens, we should more often pause to admire the brilliance of the generation that conceived our democracy within a republic. In the wake of the insufficient Articles of Confederation, they balanced power amidst fierce regionalism; they assured the continuing governance power of the people; they saw the wisdom of incorporating rights that have become our cornerstone.

We must, however, also remember that every generation must vigilantly protect those rights. While designed as a living document to be updated via amendments, its foundational tenets must be respected if we are to continue to be self-governing. We, the people, are both stewards and beneficiaries of the US Constitution.

Photo credit: Jason Hornick

GRETA VAN SUSTEREN

HOST/CHIEF POLITICAL ANALYST
FULL COURT PRESS

The awesome constitutional right of free press includes the awesome responsibility to get the facts and get it right. There can be no robust debate that is essential to a democracy if you don't have the true facts and if you fear gathering those facts. The constitutional right to a free press affirmatively protects the press to do its job.

Photo courtesy of Gray TV

DR. LEANA WEN, MD, MSC

PHYSICIAN AND PUBLIC HEALTH LEADER

The equal protection clause in the Fourteenth Amendment asserts that neither the United States nor any State shall "deny to any person within its jurisdiction the equal protection of the laws." It is the role of government to treat men, women, and all its people as individuals equal in rights, responsibilities, opportunities, and freedoms. This extends to people's health and well-being, regardless of sex.

As a doctor and frontline advocate for public health, I know that access to health care is fundamental to people leading lives of dignity. This especially holds true to comprehensive reproductive health care—including the right to safe, legal abortion, which is a key component of every person's bodily autonomy, privacy, and equality. Today's constant attacks on women's health care and attempts to stigmatize reproductive health care run counter to the spirit of the equal protection clause. At a time of huge unmet need and poor health outcomes—for women's health care in particular—it is essential that all people have access to the medical services they need, without interference by government. This is key to protecting and advancing human *dignity*, as the Constitution intends.

Photo courtesy of Dr. Leana Wen

WALTER WILLIAMS

JOHN M. OLIN DISTINGUISHED PROFESSOR OF ECONOMICS GEORGE MASON UNIVERSITY

The Framers of our Constitution had an abiding distrust of government sharing. They shared Thomas Paine's vision that "Government, even in its best state, is but a necessary evil; in its worst state, an intolerable one." The great distrust that our Founders had for government can be seen in the language of our Bill of Rights. It contains phrases such as: "Congress shall not deny, or abridge," "shall not be infringed," and "nor be deprived of life, liberty, or property without due process of law." If the Framers thought they could trust Congress, why in the world would they go to such lengths to prevent Congress from violating our liberties?

I've often suggested that when we die, and if at our next destination we see anything like a Bill of Rights, we know that we're in Hell. A Bill of Rights in Heaven would be an affront to God—suggesting that He cannot be trusted.

Photo courtesy of Marjory Hawkins

Photo courtesy of Marianne Williamson

MARIANNE WILLIAMSON

AUTHOR; LECTURER

In the Jewish religion it's said that every generation must rediscover God for itself. Similarly, every generation of Americans needs to fall in love with democracy—with its audacity, its radicalism, the promise of infinite possibility that comes from a commitment to liberty and justice and equality for all. It's not enough that these principles be written on marble walls or inscribed in our Constitution; they must be written on our hearts and inscribed in our souls, or they begin to lose their moral force. As a generation, we're being forced to ask ourselves how serious, how committed we are, to a set of principles whose only ultimate life force is the breath that we breathe into them. It is as important that we be there to protect the Constitution, as that the Constitution be there to protect us.

Photo courtesy of Dweezil Zappa

DWEEZIL ZAPPA

GUITARIST; ACTOR

As kids, we learn the concept of fairness and equality from our parents and our teachers. In our kid brains, we want all things to be fair and equal. As we get older, this concept leads to disappointment when we realize life doesn't automatically make things fair or equal and that the scales of justice aren't calibrated for that result. Many of us become disgusted by what we see and experience in our world. That is why the Constitution exists and why it's so powerful. As a simple analogy, it's essentially the equivalent of a superhero coming in to save the day for everyone all at once. While some will say it's not perfect, it's the closest thing to perfection that we all know. Imagine the corruption if modern-day politicians and lawyers were to attempt to write this document now! The Constitution is the beacon of hope that connects all of us and inspires us to be the best we can be. The foundation of freedom and protection from abuse of power is something we all want and deserve. The Constitution specifically enforces this and represents so much more. It has never been more important to uphold the words written on those pages. Words matter!

COLORFUL HEROES

ELBRIDGE GERRY

Thank goodness Elbridge Gerry never had to read an employer's annual review of his work performance. He surely would have needed a stiff tankard of rum afterward: *Grumpy, suspicious, aggressive . . . makes enemies easily . . . manages to antagonize everyone with his unpredictability . . . lousy speaker.*

Make that a double, innkeeper.

It's hard to read about Gerry without wondering if history has given him a bad rep. He may have earned his reviews, but he no more expected the historical maelstrom he lived through than any of his fellow founders.

Gerry was born in Marblehead, Massachusetts, in 1744 to a family of fish exporters. He attended Harvard and put off marriage until age forty-one, whereupon he buried himself in the job and fathered twelve children. By the time the Revolution began, he was one of the richest men in New England.

When the call of duty came, he was not one to swing a saber in battle, but he was a good money man to have on the patriot's side. In 1776 Gerry became a member of the Continental Congress, where he focused his attention on military and financial matters. As Senator Mike Lee said of Gerry in his 2017 book *Written Out of History*, "He amassed enough wealth to be considered a member of the Massachusetts 'codfish aristocracy' and was a generous statesman who saw it as his duty to help finance the War for Independence and later helped pay down the debt accrued during the fighting."

Gerry continually called for better pay and equipment for Continental troops. When Parliament blocked Boston Harbor, Marblehead became a crucial port, and he organized the shipment of supplies sent from the colonies to relieve hungry Bostonians.

Still, as a delegate, the humorless Gerry—"a nervous, bird-like little person," in Lee's words—never got comfortable with some of his towel-snapping fellow founders. Benjamin Harrison, for example, once ribbed Gerry that if the two were ever caught by the British, Gerry was so small and physically lightweight that "you'll be dancing in air on the [hangman's rope] an hour after I'm gone."

If this sort of treatment ever bothered Gerry, he could always turn to Samuel Adams, who insisted that his fellow Bay Stater was, "a man of immense worth . . . If all his fellow congressmen were like Elbridge Gerry, the liberties of America would be safe against the gates of earth and hell."

Politically, Gerry was largely a moderate. His main fear was that a central government would overpower the individual states, including his own. If he cherished Massachusetts, however, its citizens didn't always return his love. He ran for governor four times before finally winning the seat in 1810.

While in office Gerry performed a bit of legendary underhandedness, the results of which we live with to this day. He helped put into effect a law dividing the state into voting districts—favorable to his own party.

Some wags observed that many of the districts' boundaries appeared so meandering that they took on the shape of salamanders. No, another corrected, *gerrymanders*.

In 1812, Gerry was elected vice president under James Madison, but the old "Marbleheader" died a year later of a heart attack at age seventy. It was reported that he "went without a struggle." Elbridge Gerry is the only signer of the Declaration buried in Washington, DC.

Opposite: James Barton Longacre, after John Vanderlyn, c. 1820
Ink wash on paper, National Portrait Gallery, Smithsonian Institution

GEORGE MASON

George Mason is at times portrayed by historians as a tiny sapling struggling in the shadow of the towering Virginia oaks Madison, Jefferson, and Washington. But that does not seem entirely right. He was something of a homebody, not at all interested in competition, one-upmanship, or the rough and tumble of the debate floor. He had no appetite, he said, "for the smiles and frowns of the great." George Mason liked hanging out with his kids—all eleven of them.

Historian Margaret Stimmann Branson summed up Mason this way: "Mason did not suffer fools gladly. Patience was not one of his hallmarks . . . [He] was bored by legislative routines. He disliked committee work. He also shunned political office whenever possible."

Not your ideal résumé for a slot in the pantheon of venerable American heroes. But it's possible to trace how Mason came by these traits.

His father drowned when the boy was nine years old. He was raised by an uncle whose home boasted a library of 1,500 books, many of them on law. At twenty-one, Mason inherited the family's massive estate, a Georgian mansion called Gunston Hall, on the Potomac River in Virginia—George Washington was a neighbor—along with its 300 slaves. He once wrote that he was "content with the blessings of a private station."

Well, who wouldn't be? But when despondency set in upon the death of his wife of twenty-three years, he sought a distraction to occupy his fertile mind, so in the early 1770s, he dipped his beak into Virginia politics. The revolutionary spirit was already in the air along the Eastern seaboard.

Mason preferred being an advisor to statesmen rather than a statesman himself, but he eventually became the author of two documents that would be the foundation not only for Virginia rule, but for the nation.

The first, written in 1774, was a proper scolding of the British overlords called the Fairfax Resolves. Here, more or less, is a paraphrase of its fiery points:

You aren't our conquerors, don't treat us like we are; you have no right to govern us by laws we didn't agree to, so we're going to live by our own; since you don't represent our interests, you can forget our paying any damn taxes.

The other document, penned in 1776, was the Virginia Declaration of Rights. You're no doubt familiar with its most weighty point: "That all men are by nature equally free and independent and have certain inherent rights . . . namely, the enjoyment of life, liberty [and the right to pursue], happiness and safety." Jefferson tucked that into his frock coat for later use in the Declaration.

In 1787 Mason spent four months in Philadelphia at the Constitutional Convention, ultimately refusing to sign the Constitution because it did not have a bill of rights. He found Philadelphia horrifyingly decadent and decided to go home, making him perhaps the very first American politician ever to claim he wanted to spend more time with his family, and maybe the last to actually mean it.

Mason was in ill health, as he had been much of his life. By 1787 he was in bad shape, and by 1792, having turned down an appointment to the Senate to live quietly at Gunston Hall, he "left the state of human life," as Martha Washington wrote to a friend. All but a modest number of "the reluctant founder's" papers disappeared.

GOUVERNEUR MORRIS.

Nat-1752. Ob.-1816.

From the painting in the National Museum, Phil^a

GOUVERNEUR MORRIS

In Philadelphia in 1787, it is said that Alexander Hamilton made a wager with fellow patriot Gouverneur Morris that Morris couldn't get the habitually formal and standoffish George Washington to lighten up a bit. Washington famously resisted familiarity and disliked being touched. Gouverneur took the bet, and in a kind of *hey, bro* gesture walked up and slapped the Father of Our Country on the shoulder, exclaiming, "My dear General, how happy I am to see you so well!" The frosty glare that Washington returned was colder than a winter night at Valley Forge. Morris lost the bet and picked up the tab for dinner.

Gouverneur Morris was apparently an acquired taste and, apart from this personal space intrusion, Washington liked and trusted him, despite the New Yorker's reputation for being a cocky popinjay. He was also a whip-smart operator who Washington said had a "lively and brilliant mind."

Morris was born in what is today the South Bronx, New York City. Tall, self-confident, and handsome, he graduated college at age sixteen and, despite the handicap of having lost a leg in a teenage carriage wreck, became a successful lawyer. When it came time to pick sides in the Revolution, Morris had a tough choice deciding to join the patriot cause—a number of his close relatives were loyalists, including his mother.

In 1776 he served with the militia, and during the Constitutional Convention proved a predictably windy speaker—he made a record 173 speeches, including passionate denunciations of slavery—and came to be known as the "Penman of the Constitution" for his lithe way with language. Morris was responsible for the preamble's fearless first three words: We the People.

In 1789 Morris decamped the colonies for Paris where Washington appointed him minister to France, but not before telling him, at arm's length no doubt, that even with his considerable abilities, his fellow founders found his style ". . . imperious, contemptuous, and disgusting to those who might happen to differ from [his] opinion." Tough love from the commander-in-chief, who nonetheless was to rely on him as his eyes and ears in Europe.

Unfortunately, Morris found Paris "perhaps as wicked a spot as exists. Incest, murder, bestiality, fraud, rapine, oppression, baseness, cruelty." He did not believe that the French possessed the temperament to duplicate what the American rebellion accomplished, an assessment that proved correct as he witnessed the worst of the French Revolution's "Reign of Terror." Making the best of things, however, Morris managed to carry on affairs with two well-born married women until (perhaps wisely) shipping home after a decade abroad.

In 1799 Morris retreated to Morrisania, his 2,000-acre family estate in the Bronx. In 1809 he married his housekeeper, evidently willing to overlook the fact that the woman had earlier been accused of murdering a child. The couple had one son.

Morrisania provided an idyllic existence for the peg-legged patriot until one day Morris was beset with a urinary tract blockage. In an ill-advised attempt to alleviate the logjam, Morris used a piece of whalebone as a catheter. It's safe to say that this courageous and pioneering medical procedure did not survive. And neither did Morris. He died of a resulting infection at the age of sixty-one.

Opposite: http://digitalcollections.nypl.org/items/510d47db-1832-a3d9-e040-e00a18064a99 | title= (still image) Gouverneur Morris., (1863) }} |author=Digital Collections, The New York Public Library | publisher=The New York Public Library, Astor, Lennox, and Tilden Foundation}}</ref>]

JOHN RUTLEDGE

Long before the cold day that John Rutledge leapt into Charleston Bay seeking to end his life, he had endured much. He had survived the Revolutionary War. There were ten children to raise. There was endless commuting from his native South Carolina to Philadelphia and New York to hammer out the new nation's guiding documents. For the better part of thirty years, Rutledge had toiled in the building of South Carolina and the United States, having served in duties judicial, legislative, and executive. At one point he chaired a Constitutional Congress group with the soul-crushing title of the Committee of Detail, which in effect put him in charge of all of the nation's important but tedious fine print. Yet he dutifully attended all committee sessions and feverishly served on five other committees besides. No, on the day John Rutledge walked off the pier in Charleston he was not out for a relaxing swim.

Rutledge served because he believed it was the duty of the well-born in society who had the most to lose. And rich he was. Raised in Charleston and educated in London and the colonies, Rutledge made a bundle early on as an attorney, while investing in plantations and slaves.

In 1761 he leapt into South Carolina politics.

The young lawyer had no strong quarrel with the British, and although he thought self-rule for the colonies was best in the long run, he didn't agitate for complete separation from Britain.

When the Red Coats marched into Charleston in 1780, however, then-Governor Rutledge quickly changed his tune. The Brits confiscated his property and tossed his brother Edward—a signer of the Declaration—in a Florida prison. In a seemingly tactless act of overreach, the British also jailed the governor's mother.

Rutledge escaped to North Carolina and made preparations to retake South Carolina, which he did the following year, even pardoning the Loyalists who had helped shoo him out. War heroics aside, it was while working with fellow colonial delegates that Rutledge's brilliance truly shone through. Representatives from the northern colonies to the first congress in New York didn't know much about their southern colleagues beyond the fact that they owned slaves. They also assumed them to be under-educated and dull-witted.

They were right on the first point and mistaken about the second. Rutledge was no pushover. His gifts of reason and elegant oratory convinced the disparate members to work together. Nor was he shy about pressing the southern states' interests. When the discussion of slavery was raised while creating the Constitution, for example, Rutledge was unbending: "If the Convention thinks that North Carolina, South Carolina, and Georgia will ever agree to the plan, unless their right to import slaves be untouched, the expectation is in vain. The people of those states will never be such fools as to give up so important an interest."

Rutledge continued to labor shaping the new United States, but the strain began to take its toll, and there was talk in later years that he was losing his grip. He lobbied George Washington for appointment as Chief Justice of the Supreme Court. When Washington gave the job to John Jay and appointed Rutledge associate justice, the normally dependable Rutledge refused to attend a single session. Jay eventually moved on to an ambassadorship, and Washington gave Rutledge the job he wanted. Inexplicably, Rutledge then delivered a speech ranting against the absent Jay. The Senate then unanimously rejected the appointment. John Adams wrote to his wife that the rejection "gave me great pain for an old friend, though I could not but think he deserved it."

The defeat drew Rutledge into a depression from which he could not recover. He never regained the fortune the British had stolen from him. Now he was broke, a pariah, and out of a job. But the South Carolina patriot did not die in the waters of Charleston Bay—he would live until 1880. He was saved from drowning by two passing slaves.

JAMES WILSON

Of the scores of men who could lay claim to being a founding father, none is more mercurial than James Wilson. It wasn't until 158 years after Wilson's death that anyone even bothered to write his biography. Charles Page Smith, the historian who took up the task, wrote that "[Wilson] was a principal architect of our nation . . . [but] his name is virtually unknown to the general public." Even his fellow historians, Smith wrote in 1956, were clueless as to who he was.

It's not that there wasn't information out there about Wilson—however scant. It's just that no one seemed to know what to do with him. Smith pondered this and concluded that Wilson was "an enigma" who led "a prickly life, a gnarled and knotted life, hard to grasp, yielding its meaning and its humanness with reluctance, a mollusk-like life with an almost impenetrable shell . . . that [resisted] the historian's sucking knife to the end."

Wilson was born in Scotland, one of seven children. Flinty, dour, and nearsighted, he was probably not inclined to care much for the Crown even before he lit out for the colonies in 1765. He studied law in Philadelphia, then hung out his shingle in Reading, Pennsylvania. He married, fathered six children, and hit it rich as a land speculator on the frontier. Wilson was living the American dream even before there was an America.

Now an aristocrat, Wilson dove into Pennsylvania politics and was elected to the Continental Congress in 1775. He was not always on the right side of history—he insisted that women would never have what it takes to handle voting—but no one doubted his passion and his eventual willingness to compromise. "Energy," "enthusiasm," and "vitality" are words his biographer used to describe the qualities Wilson brought to debate floor. He signed the Declaration of Independence largely based upon his belief that the course of the new United States government would be determined by ordinary citizens in popular elections, not by Parliamentarians in London who had no skin in the game.

In 1789, George Washington appointed Wilson to the Supreme Court, a body that Wilson helped create. "To Wilson must also go much credit for the conception of the Supreme Court," wrote his biographer. He expected to be named Chief Justice but was seated as only an associate judge. It was about this time that his American dream began to take a dark turn.

He proved a lackadaisical jurist who wrote few opinions. But there were other stressors in his life. A widower, he had remarried and fathered a child who died in infancy. Most pressing, however, were the debts he had accrued in land deals gone bad—Wilson's "ardent speculations," John Adams called them—which only worsened with the Panic of 1796.

Wilson attempted to influence legislation that would benefit land speculators in Pennsylvania. No one would deny that when you are a sitting Supreme Court justice, this sort of thing just doesn't look good.

Eventually, Wilson landed in debtor's prison in New Jersey. Upon release he fled to North Carolina, dodging his creditors. "Hunted like a wild beast," he wrote.

Wilson died in North Carolina of malaria (according to some accounts), or of a stroke. In any case, to his fellow justices, one of whom bought his Supreme Court robe for $17 after he was gone, Wilson had become an embarrassment and likely would have been impeached had he lived. His death did them all a favor.

Biographer Smith portrays Wilson more charitably as a man with the same human weaknesses and strengths as any other of his fellow founders. James Wilson's is, he wrote, "the story of a Scottish farm boy who, in seeking his fortune, helped to create ours."

FUN CONSTITUTIONAL FACTS

Poor Prophecy: Walking with a friend some time before the close of the Constitutional Convention in 1787, Washington lamented, "I do not expect the Constitution to last for more than twenty years."

Autocorrect?: "Pensylvania" isn't a typo next to one signer's name. That was how the state was spelled at the time.

Pest Control: Patrick Henry refused a position as a delegate because he "smelt a rat."

And No Overtime: Delegates debated from 10 a.m. to 3 p.m. six days a week. They had only a ten-day break during the convention, May 25, 1787 to September 17, 1787. The "committee of the whole" actually debated for about eighty-eight days.

A Walk About Paris: Thomas Jefferson could not sign the Constitution. He was in France, serving as US minister.

And London: John Adams did not sign it either. He served as US minister to Great Britain during the Constitutional Convention.

Perfect Attendance: James Madison is the only delegate who attended every meeting.

Ink Master: Pennsylvania General Assembly Clerk Jacob Shallus received a $30 calligraphy fee for the actual penning of the document.

Cussin' Commander: During the Battle of Monmouth in 1778, normally mild-mannered George Washington used so much profanity that nearby General Charles Scott said the future president swore "until leaves shook on the tree. [I] have never enjoyed such swearing before or since."

Date Stamp: September 17 is Constitution Day, marking the day the framers signed the document.

All in Favor: Seventy-five delegates were invited to participate; fifty-five actually did. Though forty-two delegates attended the Constitutional Convention on signing day, only thirty-nine signed it.

Just Said No: George Mason and Elbridge Gerry didn't sign the Constitution because it lacked a Bill of Rights. Edmund Randolph didn't sign, but eventually supported ratification of the document. All three were staunch Anti-Federalists who wanted to protect states' and individuals' rights.

Assisted Living: Benjamin Franklin needed help signing the Constitution due to poor health. He was the oldest signer at eighty-one years of age. He was carried into meetings on a chair borne by four prisoners.

Good Kid: Jonathan Dayton of New Jersey was the youngest signer at twenty-six years old.

Bad Kid: James Madison's stepson John Payne Todd—Dolley's boy from her first marriage—proved to be a lout interested only in gambling, drinking, and money. Paying off his debts nearly ruined Madison financially.

Presidential Signers: George Washington and James Madison were the only (future) presidents to sign.

Double Signers: Six men signed both the Declaration of Independence and the Constitution: George Read, Roger Sherman, Benjamin Franklin, Robert Morris, George Clymer, and James Wilson.

Who's a Voter?: The Constitution doesn't say. At first, only white male property owners had the vote.

Name the Framers: The Founding Fathers never heard the words "Founding Fathers." The term didn't come into use until 1916 when then-Senator Warren G. Harding used it in a speech at the Republican National Convention. Membership in the club included men who fought in the American Revolution, drafters of the Constitution, and signers of the Declaration of Independence.

Art of Compromise: Some wanted representation based on population. Other delegates argued for equal representation for each state. We ended up with both the House (population representation) and the Senate (equal representation) in the Great Compromise, devised by Roger Sherman of Connecticut.

Founders Will Debate Anything: One night in 1776 John Adams and Benjamin Franklin were forced to share a hotel room on the road. Franklin argued for the health benefits of leaving the window open; Adams believed they'd catch colds. Franklin won.

Slavery: The word "slavery" doesn't appear in the original Constitution. (Not until the Thirteenth Amendment, which abolished it.) The institution of slavery was, reflected, however, in the Three-Fifths Compromise. The compromise limited southern states' power in the House of Representatives by allowing them to count only 3/5 of those "bound to service for a term of years" (indentured servants) and "all other Persons" (meaning slaves).

But Trending Upward: At the time of the Constitution's signing, the entire population of the United States was roughly 4 million.

Question, Madam?: Benjamin Franklin, when asked by a woman what kind of government the framers had created, replied, "A republic, madam. If you can keep it."

Trigger Word: The word "democracy" cannot be found in the Constitution. The Framers were wary of democracy because it meant mob rule.

Ch-Ch-Changes I: The Constitution has been changed only seventeen times since 1791. A change requires enacting an amendment. (There are more than seventeen amendments, but the first ten, known as the Bill of Rights,were added as a group.) More than 11,000 amendments have been proposed, but only twenty-seven ratified.

Ch-Ch-Changes II: Benjamin Franklin didn't always toe the party line regarding liberty and independence. In 1725, at age nineteen, he self-published a pamphlet entitled *A Dissertation Upon Liberty and Necessity, Pleasure and Pain* arguing that humans didn't actually have free will. When he was older and wiser he burned every copy of the pamphlet he could find.

Thanks for the Memories: When Congress ordered a record of the Convention published in 1818, then-Secretary of State John Quincy Adams discovered that the notes of Convention Secretary William Jackson were incomplete. He reached out to other attendees in order to fill in the gaps.

Wage Freeze: Proposed in 1789 but not ratified until 1992, the Twenty-seventh Amendment (originally the second proposed amendment) states that changes in Senate and Congressional compensation cannot take effect until after another election has taken place.

Turkey Call: George Washington declared Thursday, November 26, 1789 a day of thanks observed by the People of the United States for the establishment of "a form of government for their safety and happiness."

Snail Mail: Thomas Jefferson, though absent from the convention, was still aware of its progress. In fact, he even sent his own rough version to the Convention. It arrived mere days after the Constitution had already been signed. Jefferson's draft was alike in many ways but also had some significant differences including protection for land ownership by Native Americans and a ban on slavery.

Term Limits: Jefferson believed that unless a term limit were imposed it was possible that some politicians would seek to become "an officer for life."

What's in a Name?: Nine of the fifty-five Convention attendees were named William; three of the Georgia representatives were Williams; five Convention attendees were named George.

But There Was Only One Otis: John Adams credited forgotten founder James Otis Jr. with first uttering the phrase "taxation without representation is tyranny." Maybe, maybe not. Otis was strange and unstable. He would sometimes argue a case and then immediately reverse himself in the same speech. According to historian John L. Smith, "He challenged a custom commissioner to a fight outside a coffeehouse, where Otis had the snot beaten out of him." Otis died in 1783 when a bolt of lightning killed him standing in an Andover house doorway.

Capital Cases: Before the Constitution, we were the united States of America—thirteen allied but separate governments. Under the governmental structure created by the Constitution, we became the United States of America—one nation. A big difference signified with one capital letter.

Can You Break a 5,000?: Until it was discontinued in 1946, James Madison's portrait appeared on the $5,000 bill.

The More Things Change . . .: Washington was the first president, of many, to decry fake news. In 1792 he wrote to a colleague that he was tired of newspapers exaggerating the nation's political discontent. He complained that "this kind of representation is an evil which must be placed in opposition to the infinite benefits resulting from a free press."

APPENDIX

PRODUCTION NOTES, *A MORE OR LESS PERFECT UNION*

As Senior Executive Producer at Free To Choose Network and Executive Producer (together with Bob Chitester and Rob Chatfield) of our landmark public television series on the American Constitution featuring Judge Douglas Ginsburg, I was privileged to work closely with the extraordinary production team of Barbara Potter and Jim Taylor, aided by the excellent writing and co-producing of Gary Parker. This remarkable series is the tenth project that Barbara and Jim and I have created together at Free To Choose Network and follows a productive relationship that began twenty-five years earlier with programs and series for the Discovery Networks, A&E, and Turner Broadcasting. Now as then, the hallmark of the Potter/Taylor team has always been programs and series of imaginative, high-quality production values; *A More or Less Perfect Union* most certainly continues and expands that tradition, as does this remarkable collection of thoughts on the Constitution and its importance from seventy-one distinguished Americans.

We began this far-reaching project nearly three years ago with only two essential building blocks: the universal feeling at Free To Choose Network that there was a great and timely need for a new understanding of the US Constitution as the document that "governs the laws that govern us" and Judge Douglas Ginsburg's agreement to devote a major portion of his time, knowledge, and energy to a project unlike anything he had done before. As it turns out, Doug's easy manner made him a natural for the camera. But it was the trust that developed over the past three years between Barbara Potter, Jim Taylor, and Judge Ginsburg that became the basis of our success.

From the beginning, we sought to create a lively, upbeat, and contemporary series devoid of the academic stereotypes one might expect in a project on "the Constitution." There were meetings and meetings and meetings. There were, of course, multiple drafts of ideas—some good and some rejected out of hand. Every idea was fair game with the project team. Finally, with the excellent help of Max Borders and Randy Barnett, the project began to come together as an extensive list of participants representing a broad political and academic spectrum agreed to participate. Simultaneously, there were lengthy and intensive sessions with Doug Ginsburg to fashion the stories, the production locations, and the techniques that would bring the programs to life. Throughout the research and preproduction process, Barbara Potter created regular production progress reports for me and others at Free To Choose. What follows might be called "The Anatomy of a Television Series." The text is excerpted from Barbara's progress reports documenting the process of evolution by which *A More or Less Perfect Union* was carefully created to appeal to as broad an audience as possible. It will be presented on PBS in early 2020 by our partners at WNET in New York.

After extensive preliminary research, numerous meetings with Judge Ginsburg and others, and obtaining the necessary production permissions, the project began in earnest in January 2017. The following excerpts from Barbara Potter's progress reports track the production of the series from April 2017 to August 2019.

—**Thomas Skinner, executive producer**

PRODUCER'S PROGRESS REPORT #1: APRIL 2017

Collecting Interviews: Since January we have all but completed our interviews with the many authorities that will be featured throughout the three programs. Primary filming began mid-April. The crew was in DC, New York, Chicago, and Atlanta, interviewing historians, scholars, and other constitutional experts in a variety of locations. We had wonderful cooperation wherever we went—at universities like George Mason, George Washington, Chicago, and Yale, at the Brookings Institute and the Federalist Society, and in offices, like the headquarters of the Institute for Justice. The interviews were lengthy and extremely thorough, addressing each person's area of expertise as well as some general questions about American history and the Constitution. Every interview was different, interesting, and very useful to our project.

Scripting: Our scriptwriter and co-producer, Gary Parker, has been working closely with director Jim Taylor to finalize the scripts and further develop the visuals. As the interviews were completed they were transcribed and sent, with a QuickTime movie, to Gary for review and editing. Based on the script outline, he chose the best segments from each interview, which were edited together to form a realistic audio framework for each of the three programs. The scripts are being fact-checked at FTCM as the final story research is being completed. Shooting began again in mid-April and will continue through fall.

Location Production: Whitney Plantation

This fully restored indigo plantation in Wallace, Louisiana, has been recently opened to the public as the only plantation museum in the country completely devoted to slavery. The antebellum mansion, outbuildings, and slave cabins appear much the same as they did during the plantation's pre-Civil War period. The property provides a vision of the lives and suffering of enslaved people in this country during the nineteenth century and serves as a memorial to them. Senegalese Director of Research Dr. Ibrahima Seck accompanied us during our two-day shoot. He has spent the last seventeen years researching the names and stories of the hundreds of enslaved people who spent their lives at the Whitney Plantation. We also met and interviewed Sybil Morial, a direct descendant of a domestic slave and the Whitney Plantation owner's brother. It's important to communicate the conditions of slavery in America before the Civil War to our audience.

Location Production: *Plessy v. Ferguson*

One of the most important civil rights Supreme Court cases in history was *Plessy v. Ferguson*. We decided to tell the story through the words of their descendants. In the 1890s, in New Orleans, Homer Plessy was a shoemaker who was one-eighth African American. To challenge the legality of the Louisiana "Separate Car Act," he bought a ticket and rode in a "Whites Only" train car. He was arrested and his case was heard by Louisiana Judge John Ferguson, who ruled against him. The case eventually ended up in the Supreme Court and, instead of overturning the state law, the Supreme Court established the nationwide principle of "separate but equal." Homer Plessy's relative, Keith Plessy, and Judge Ferguson's great-great-granddaughter, Phoebe Ferguson, live in New Orleans. They have created an organization—the Plessy and Ferguson Foundation—to educate people about the

Dr. Ibrahima Seck, Whitney Plantation Director of Research

Civil Rights movement and the historic events that were part of it. We spent a full day filming with them, hearing about their families' reconciliation and the important educational work of their foundation.

A Partial List of Production Sequences Scheduled for Spring/ Summer 2017: In late May we will shoot inside Independence Hall in Philadelphia. We have hired a group of Framer re-enactors to work with us, including men who portray Benjamin Franklin, James Madison, Alexander Hamilton, George Washington, and George Mason. As experienced historians themselves, they will assume their character roles for a dialogue with Judge Ginsburg. We have been approved for a shooting permit by the National Park Service (managers of Independence Hall) and plan to

George Mason, Alexander Hamilton, Barbara Potter, Doug Ginsburg, James Madison, Jim Taylor, and Ben Franklin at Independence Hall

spend two days and evenings shooting exteriors and interiors there, with and without visitors present. We have also hired a professional courtroom sketch artist who will draw some of the important characters not represented in archival artwork of the Convention. While in Philadelphia, Judge Ginsburg will interact with tourists and discuss their opinions of the Constitution. He will be there with us for two days.

Mount Vernon, Monticello, and Montpelier: We have been working with all three of these historic homes in Virginia to arrange exterior and interior shooting. Each is run by a different foundation and has different requirements and regulations associated with filming permissions and rights. They are especially concerned with the priceless antiques and artifacts on display throughout the houses. We have received permission to film exteriors and interiors at all three of these properties. Judge Ginsburg will accompany us to Monticello and Montpelier in May.

Civil War Event: Every July, an enormous Battle of Gettysburg re-enactment takes place over a three-day period. We have arranged to shoot there with Judge Ginsburg and have been given permission to interview the soldiers and talk with the visitors at the encampments and anywhere on site.

Revolutionary War Event: We will be in Sturbridge Village, Massachusetts, for the annual "Redcoats and Rebels" re-enactment weekend in August. Along with battle scenes, we'll also be shooting some special vignettes with a few soldiers who will work with us off the battlefield to evoke Shay's Rebellion and the Third Amendment's prohibition against the quartering of troops in private houses. Judge Ginsburg will accompany us to Sturbridge.

The *Dred Scott* Decision: Lynne Jackson is the great-great-granddaughter of Dred and Harriet Scott, two enslaved people who went to the Supreme Court to sue for their freedom and lost. The Court claimed that no Black person could claim US citizenship. This landmark decision is cited as one of the causes of the Civil War, which began three years later. We will visit Ms. Jackson in June in her hometown of St. Louis and hear the family's story as we see her photos and accompany her to sites that evoke the case. Today she is president of the Dred Scott Heritage Foundation. In March, a descendant of Judge Taney, the judge who wrote the *Dred Scott* decision, apologized to Ms. Jackson and her family in a formal reconciliation ceremony, 160 years after the trial.

Free Speech Challenges: Hour three will open with a stand-up comedian performing his routine about political correctness and the current climate challenging free speech. We've identified and contacted a popular young comic who is thrilled to work with us. He is booking a club in Charleston, South Carolina, and will adapt his material to fit our needs. He will find that there's a full audience. We'll also interview him about his view of free speech and the Constitution.

Archival Material Research: We have hired Lisa Hartjens, a film archivist based in Washington, DC. She specializes in researching material from the US National Archives and Library of Congress and has had extensive experience as the lead researcher on many documentaries and will source all relevant material for our program.

Next Steps and Schedule: Production will continue throughout the summer and fall. As mentioned above, Judge Ginsburg will accompany the crew to some of the historic locations and events, including Independence Hall, Monticello, Montpelier, Sturbridge Village, and Gettysburg. He will also do most of the interviewing of people on the street in various locations in and around Washington.

PRODUCER'S PROGRESS REPORT #2:

This spring and summer, we have shot much of the primary material researched between January and April. We have also begun the process of organizing the newly shot material for future editing.

Civil War Event at Gettysburg: We attended the enormous re-enactment of the Battle of Gettysburg. We shot for three humid days, documenting every aspect of the event. There were more than a thousand participants. Judge Ginsburg accompanied us, interviewing the soldiers and talking with visitors at the encampments and elsewhere on site about the Constitution and the events leading up to the Civil War. We even met and interviewed General Ulysses S. Grant's great-great-grandson.

Revolutionary War Event at Old Sturbridge Village: We spent a weekend at the annual "Redcoats and Rebels" re-enactment weekend in Sturbridge, Massachusetts, in August. In addition to the battle scenes, we also captured some special vignettes with soldiers who worked with us, off the battlefield, to evoke Shay's Rebellion and the Third Amendment's prohibition against the quartering of troops in private houses. We took advantage of being in this colonial town and used some of the historic buildings as backdrops for these special scenes. Judge Ginsburg was with us and talked with a number of the soldiers and officers, as well as delivered portions of the script to camera.

Next Steps and Schedule: Shooting will continue throughout the fall in DC, Paris, and London, where we have special permission to film one of the four copies of the Magna Carta.

PRODUCER'S PROGRESS REPORT #3:

Urban Scenes (New York): We worked with a diverse group of college students in New York City to illustrate First Amendment rights through a series of dramatic vignettes. The scenes took place in a park, in a small store, in front of a church, and on the streets. FTC friend Tanvir Toy helped us find actors and locations in the city and coordinate the shoot.

Colonial Williamsburg (Virginia): We spent a day at Colonial Williamsburg, shooting interiors and exteriors with Judge Ginsburg on camera. We had access to the Village and interiors of buildings like the House of Burgesses and the Governor's Palace. We talked to visitors on the grounds and a few docents in their workshops.

Eminent Domain (New Jersey): In Atlantic City, New Jersey, we filmed a sequence with Charlie Birnbaum, whose longtime family home is being seized through eminent domain for part of a casino development plan. This case, represented by the Institute for Justice, has been in and out of court for a few years and is in the process of being appealed again. Birnbaum's house is one of the very few left standing after most of his neighborhood was torn down for a bankrupt urban renewal project to benefit the Casino Development Authority of Atlantic City. Charlie says that this is an abuse of eminent domain and vows to fight on.

Washington, DC: We spent several days with Judge Ginsburg in various locations around DC and Baltimore, including in front of the White House to talk about the powers of the president and at the Newseum, where he focused on First Amendment rights. We also filmed at the Vietnam Veterans Memorial with General George Casey, where he and Ginsburg discussed history and war. In Baltimore we walked through the neighborhood where Justice Thurgood Marshall grew up and Doug talked about his

Printshop at Colonial Williamsburg

relationship with Marshall and how he became the first African American Supreme Court justice.

UK: We had a very special opportunity to film Judge Ginsburg with the Magna Carta at Guildhall in London. Matthew Richardson, a London City alderman, is a friend of Doug's and was able to bring the 1257 document to a historic meeting room where we had it all to ourselves. It was an amazing experience. The alderman even took the Plexiglas off for a few minutes so that we could get a shot of the document without any glare. We then shot around Guildhall and visited the Magna Carta Memorial in Runnymede.

In Essex, England, we went to see Peter Grimwood, a man who designs and crafts orreries, the fascinating devices that demonstrate how our planetary system operates. The Framers imagined the three branches of government balancing one another in a similar fashion.

France: We went to Paris to shoot evocative scenes of Thomas Jefferson's time there, before and during the Constitutional Convention, when he served as the US ambassador to France.

At the Archives with the Constitution

While there, he collected hundreds of books that were not available in the US and shipped them to his friend James Madison in Virginia. We arranged to shoot point-of-view material at a number of antique bookstores and at the fabulous library of the National Assembly in Paris. We rented an antique leather trunk and placed it in an ornate room and filled it with books as Jefferson had.

Jefferson packing books to send to Madison

Dressing our audio engineer for the Jefferson book scene in Paris

In Paris at the National Library

Fall Shooting

Shooting continued throughout October in DC, Charleston, and Savannah. We also spent a day with Judge Ginsburg at the National Constitution Center in Philadelphia.

Judge Ginsburg with James Madison at National Constitution Center

PRODUCER'S FINAL PROGRESS REPORT #4

The last days of shooting covered a bit of everything. We attended a naturalization oath ceremony at beautiful Faneuil Hall in Boston with Judge Ginsburg. There were 379 candidates for citizenship from over fifty countries. Along with their family members, they filled the historic hall. Afterward, we talked with some of the new Americans about how they feel now and what the Constitution means to them. They had all studied American history and passed a civics test before they could take the oath of citizenship. It touched all of us to be there. In order to be allowed to shoot, we had to go through a lengthy security and permit process with the Department of Homeland Security. Once we were finally granted permission, we had to find a location that was photogenic and contact the presiding judge who made the final decision. We received several rejections before striking gold!

Interviewing new citizen after naturalization ceremony

Actors in NY filming opening to Episode 2

We also shot with Judge Ginsburg in Washington, DC, and Virginia. We went to a historic courthouse in Loudoun County, Virginia, to talk about plea bargaining and to a red barn, at a remote farm found through an online search, to enhance our segment about the Supreme Court case, *Wickard v. Filburn*. This was a 1942 case about a small farmer who grew extra feed for his animals, which resulted in a big increase of regulatory power for the Federal Government. In DC we returned to the Newseum to cover more information about the First Amendment. The Newseum is a fantastic place, devoted to teaching about First Amendment issues throughout history, and each day displays the front pages of hundreds of newspapers from around the country. And there's a perfect view of the Capitol's dome from their roof deck. They have been very welcoming to our crew and supportive of our project.

This fall we've also shot in New York to gather B-roll for some montages and visuals to match specific copy in each of our episodes. We hired several actors to work with us on short scenes illustrating some aspects of the Sedition Act of 1917. For instance, speaking out against the government was prohibited in the press, as was anti-draft leafleting, so we printed leaflets appealing to young men not to register for the draft and handed them to passersby on a city sidewalk. Using graphics, we will show that this was BANNED. Remaining to be filmed are short B-roll shots to support several narrative points in a few other places.

POSTPRODUCTION

Editing

There are over 135 hours of originally shot, raw material for this series. The culling of all interviews, supporting stories, and B-roll footage has been completed and rough assemblages of all three hours are complete. The first, very rough versions were longer and more loosely edited than what is now being accomplished. In this second round of editing, the narration and interviews are becoming more precise, the archival holes are being filled with temporary or permanent images, music is added, and the transitions between segments are becoming smoother. This more refined version of hour one has been finished and the second hour is underway. Fine cutting of all three shows will continue through spring.

Music

We've met with John Keltonic, the composer who will create the music for the programs, and screened the first episode with him. We discussed music styles and placement and he has since sent us some short compositions to try over several scenes. He is continually working on our project and in touch weekly. This process will take several months.

Graphics

There will be many graphic elements in each episode. Working with a designer, we have developed a graphic look or "signature" for the series. The title will be bold and will evoke the Constitution and our Republic. Each of the three hours will have the same main title plus an individual name for the episode. Using the same colors, we will develop "lower thirds" with the names and titles of our many distinguished experts and participants, location identifiers, and phrasing from the Constitution to be superimposed or scrolled on screen. The look is clean and bold.

Archival Research

Each of the three episodes, particularly the first two, feature archival still and moving images. We have been researching sources and licenses for this material with the help of a professional film archivist. We're using paintings and prints, photographs and film footage, documents and reproductions of all kinds. Some of them are in the National Archives and the Library of Congress, but many are in private collections or owned by stock film companies and broadcasters. For example, the best portrait of Isaac Newton is in the US Senate collection and must be requested from them. Finding the highest resolution images and licensing them for use is a very time-consuming process and will continue throughout the post-production.

IN CONCLUSION

With the three programs now finished and all of the necessary approvals in place, *A More or Less Perfect Union* will receive its initial distribution in January 2020 via PBS. It will be presented to the nation's public television stations by WNET/Thirteen in New York. Subsequent distributions will follow.

The crew at the pub after a long day.

ACKNOWLEDGMENTS

Marley Behrendt
Robert Chatfield
Patrick Cooke
Susan Gable
Susan Gold
Mike Hanel
Marjory Hawkins
Len Juniewicz
Michael Kraus
Joe Lehr
Amy Ritzel
Dana Roberts
Tara L. Schupp

FREE TO CHOOSE NETWORK

Free To Choose Network is a 501(c)3 global entertainment company which produces thought-provoking documentaries, offering diverse voices, powerful stories, and a fresh perspective on a range of important global and national issues through its production company, Free To Choose Media. For more than forty years, the Free To Choose production teams have traveled the world to explore topics such as the economic roots of the Arab Spring and the inspiring stories of entrepreneurs raising themselves and their communities out of poverty, as well as revealing how innovation and new technologies may be the answer to the world's growing energy needs. For more information, visit the website at www.FreeToChooseNetwork.org.

RESOURCES

*Denotes Fun Facts resources

WEBSITES

nationalarchives.org
explorethearchive.com
thehistoryjunkie.com
history.com
forbes.com
*constitutionfacts.com
quora.com
allthingsliberty.com
howstuffworks.com
businessinsider.com
ranker.com
huffpost.com
*mentalfloss.com
marksquotes.com
foundingfatherquotes.com
wordpress.com
*biography.com
american.revolution.com
biographyyourdictionary.com
mountvernon.org
bookstellyouwhy.com
let.rug.nl/usa/biographies
goodreads.com
conservipedia.com
revolutionarywar.com
civiced.org
jstor.org

BOOKS

James Wilson: Founding Father, 1742-1798, by Charles Page Smith; University of North Carolina Press, 1956
Written Out of History, by Senator Mike Lee, Random House; 2017
The Life of Elbridge Gerry, by James Trecothick Austin; Applewood Books; 1828
The Signers, by Dennis Brindell Fradin; Bloomsbury; 2002
**Washington: A Life,* by Ron Chernow; Penguin; 2010
The Framer's Coup: The Making of the U.S. Constitution, by Michael J. Klarman; Oxford; 2016

Vindicating the Founders: Race, Sex, Class and Justice in the Origins of America, by Thomas G. West; Rowman & Littlefield; 1997
The Intimate Lives of the Founding Fathers, by Thomas Fleming; Smithsonian Books; 2009
Revolutionaries: A New History of the Invention of America, by Jack Rakove; Houghton Mifflin Harcourt; 2010
Founding Father: Rediscovering George Washington, by Richard Brookhiser; Simon & Schuster Inc.; 1996

INDEX